Chakra Yoga Cleanse

Journey Through the Rainbow Bridge

To Jaishree,
Love & Blessings on your
Journey. Namaste,
Sharon xx ♡ xx

Ayurvedic Yoga Lifestyle

https://heavenonearth.space/chakra-cleanse/

E-mail: sharon@heavenonearth.space

ISBN: 978-0-9956742-1-9

AUTHOR'S DISCLAIMER: The contents of this book are the opinions of the author. This book contains general information about nutrition, health and diets and is not designed to replace your regular physician. Consult with a qualified health practitioner before beginning your cleanse.

Editor: Gill Prior
email: gillian.prior@hotmail.co.uk

Printed by Book Printing UK
Remus House, Coltsfoot Drive, Peterborough, PE2 9BF

Book Printing UK takes our environmental responsibility very seriously. All of the paper used is FSC credited, which means that it has been sourced responsibly by organisations who ensure that they are re-planting trees to replace those that they use.

Dear Reader,

Welcome to the Chakra Yoga Cleanse. Thank you for choosing this book to help you on your path to ascension. I am truly grateful for the opportunity to guide you on a journey of transformation and realisation of the true Self.

As a Gatekeeper of the New Earth, it is my purpose and mission to assist the collective awakening of humanity.

I honour and respect the Divine Being that you are, and I am here for you every step of the way. Namaste.

This book is dedicated to all the souls brave and courageous enough to do the inner work, and who devote themselves to the spiritual path towards truth and freedom.

It is time to ascend the Rainbow Bridge and manifest Heaven on Earth.

It is your time to Shine!

Contents

PART 1 – THEORY

Introduction – Discovering Your Superhuman Abilities

We live in a magical world where anything is possible...

The Chakra Yoga Cleanse will take you on a voyage of discovery deep into your heart and soul where you will uncover the gifts and magic inside you.

On a journey like no other, you will step out of the ordinary and into extraordinary to experience a life of pure beauty and ecstatic bliss.

The Chakra Yoga Cleanse is a journey through the Rainbow Bridge, guiding you, the reader, to cleanse your subtle body and ultimately manifest Heaven on Earth.

By committing to a daily sadhana (spiritual practice), you will elevate your energy and restore balance and harmony to your body, mind, heart and soul.

When connecting with our energy body and working with the chakras, we tap into the limitless potential of the Universe and realise that anything is possible.

Do you realise how amazingly powerful you are?

Magic is not something we create out of thin air; it is who we are at our core. We have untapped streams of limitless energy hidden within our body waiting to be discovered.

Once you align your thoughts, feelings and actions, you can quite literally manifest anything you desire.

The physical world which we see with our physical eyes is merely a fraction of our existence in this universe, which is a fraction of the multiverse. Quantum physics has discovered what the ancient yogis always knew. Noetic science studies objective scientific tools and techniques combined with subjective inner knowing and intuition to explore the nature of reality and consciousness. Every human on this planet is powerful beyond measure, and you are no exception. You were born for greatness and to make a difference in the world.

There are many dimensions of existence that are available to us when we open up to our Divine nature and multidimensionality.

On remembrance of who we are, and why we are here, we wake up from the illusion of separation and step into wholeness. We remember we are sovereign beings with dormant potential residing deep within us.

This is the beginning of our journey...

Welcome to the 5th Dimension!

Soul wisdom from all our previous life experiences sleeps within the DNA strands, waiting to be woken up and revealed. Many eons ago when we first came to Earth, our bodies were not solid and dense as they are today. The physical body was originally created from the etheric realms. Overtime, we slowly built a garment of flesh around our Light Body. Dark forces in the world altered human DNA to reduce the amount of light in our bodies, which enabled them to install programmes that would have detrimental effects on physical, mental and emotional health, and also decrease spiritual awareness.

We are on the verge of a massive shift in consciousness. As the planet elevates to higher frequencies, souls who are awake on this journey are absorbing the light and changing at a cellular level. Our bodies are transforming back to our natural crystalline state of being.

Listen to the whispering of your heart calling you,
Listen to that inner voice
You are being called to go within,
The inward path to self-realisation and self-mastery

Before we come to Earth, we are assigned a mission to fulfil; we sign a soul contract with the Celestial Council. Our memories are wiped clear when we are born; we have amnesia and forget why we have come to Earth. We get distracted by the world around us through our sensory pleasures and forget our mission and purpose for this incarnation. Lost in the illusion of the physical world, we move further away from our Divine nature, caught up in the physical realms of the Earthly plane. It is our responsibility to find our way back to Source and align with universal consciousness.

Have you travelled so far away from yourself that you have forgotten who you are?

We are all here for a reason, with a purpose and mission to fulfil. To uncover your purpose in this life time, follow your passion, and follow your heart, it will lead you to your destiny.

Mother Earth is ascending, and she gently ushers us to do the same. By listening to the sounds of nature, and tuning into your intuition, you will arrive back home, to the heart of your true Self. Physical, mental and emotional suffering are the entry points into higher states of awareness. Our body sends us signals through pain, to guide us back into the light of Oneness with Great Spirit. When we listen to those messages, and then take action on the guidance that comes through intuitively, we bring ourselves back into alignment.

As we move through this ascension collectively, we are transitioning from the 3rd dimension into the 5th dimension and beyond. Dimensions are different states of consciousness and are accessible to anyone at any time. The main purpose of this book is to help humanity shift into higher dimensions of peace, love and harmony, which can be equated to the 5th dimension.

The theory section of this book will give you an understanding of the techniques used on the Chakra Yoga Cleanse and the significant healing potential of yoga for ultimate health and wellbeing of body, mind, heart and soul.

The 3rd dimensional world we live in is dualistic, everything is governed by opposites; yin/yang, male/female, darkness/light, spirit/matter etc. We live our lives through polarity. Without feeling sad, how can we know what it feels like to be happy? If we have never experienced pain, how would we appreciate pleasure? We are here to experience life as a human being, and part of that experience is to understand the polarity of opposites. The 3rd dimension is governed by maya, the illusion of the physical world. It is unpredictable and not what it appears to be. We live in a universe of great mystery and magic. When we recognise the world with maya at the surface, we can discover the depths of true beauty and cosmic reality wherever we look. This realisation elevates our consciousness, and we evolve spiritually.

The physical element of us is HUMAN
Connecting us to the 3rd dimension and the Earth

We need the density of the 3rd dimension to manifest things into material form within physical reality. When we wake up from the illusion that we are separate and realise there is more to life than the physical world, we enter into the 4th dimension, the astral realm where all possibilities live in the infinite field of consciousness.

In the 5th dimension, we transcend dualism and realise that everything and everyone is connected, we are One, there is no separation. Yoga helps us to find balance between these polar opposites, to merge them together in Oneness. We experience the 5th dimension when we live fully from our hearts, manifesting Heaven on Earth through Divine unity. We move from the illusion of duality to the truth of Oneness.

The Spirit element of us is ANGELIC
Connecting us to the 5th dimension and the Heavenly Realms

We are both human and Angel, matter and Spirit. Your journey on Earth is to rediscover who you truly are, both your human nature and your Angelic Self. We are becoming lighter as our vibrations raise in frequency shifting us towards the New Earth, which is already here within our hearts and minds.

Our conscious breath is the link between Heaven and Earth, the spiritual and physical Self. When we are consciously aware of our breathing, it brings peace and balance to the nervous system, restoring our health and wellbeing.

This cleanse will guide you to find the still and silent place within where your Spirit dwells. By turning your awareness to your inner world, the spark of your eternal soul will ignite and propel you forth on your ascension, guiding you back into your heart to align with your Divine nature.

Your imagination will carry you across the veil of the physical world into the celestial realms

The practical techniques in this book will cleanse, heal and restore balance to the subtle energy body and transform your life in miraculous ways. The ancient knowledge of yoga will awaken esoteric wisdom that resides within you.

I have spent my entire life studying the mind-body connection; the complexity of the human body and mind has always fascinated me. Over the next few chapters, I will share with you my story, and how living a yoga lifestyle helped me to overcome chronic back pain, insomnia and depression, leading me to my purpose in life. I hope this book inspires you to delve deeper into your Divine essence so that you can connect with your passions and purpose.

Using the spiritual tools in this book, including yoga, meditation, energy healing, chakra balancing, aromatherapy, nutrition, sound and crystal therapy, plus more, you will feel renewed and rejuvenated physically, mentally, emotionally and spiritually.

Prepare yourself for a transformational journey through the chakras into higher states of consciousness and alternate realities as you discover your true POWER and POTENTIAL!

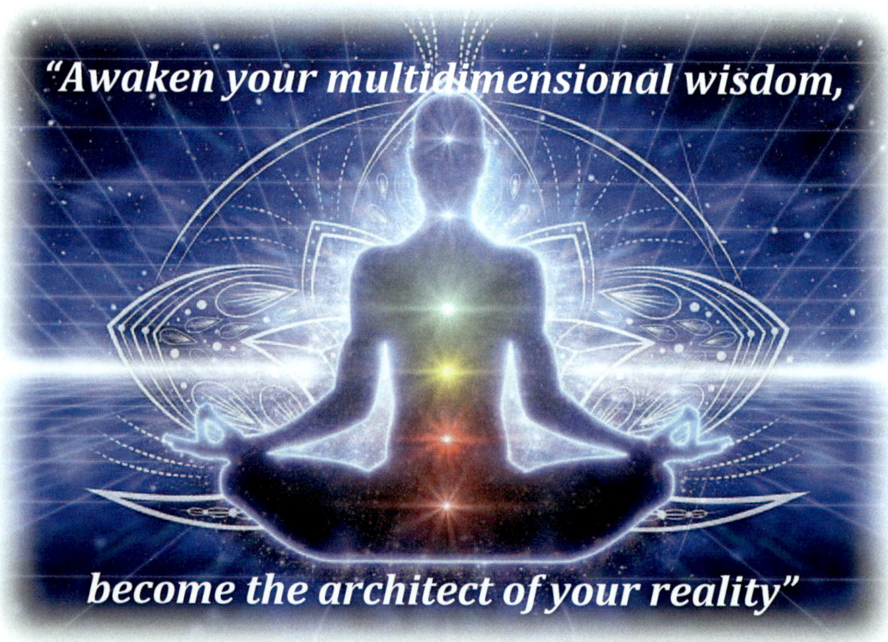

Chapter 1: Yoga – A Path to Freedom

What is Yoga?

Yoga comes from the Sanskrit word 'yuj' which means 'to yoke' or 'to join'. It is a complete science that connects the individual Self to universal consciousness.

Yoga is a physical, mental, emotional and spiritual practice that unites body, mind, heart and Spirit. The ultimate goal of yoga is self-development and self-realisation. Yoga is a journey to help us remember who we are and why we are here. It is a pathway for us to find inner peace and freedom, to experience Heaven on Earth.

The Healing Power of Yoga

Yoga has tremendous power to transform our lives in unimaginable ways!

Anything is possible when you believe!

After breaking my back, I thought I would never walk properly again let alone get back into kickboxing! I suffered with chronic pain for 7 years before committing to a daily yoga practice and healing myself completely. 3 years after my full recovery, I fulfilled a life-long dream of going to Thailand to stay on a Muay Thai boot camp training intensely with professional fighters every day for a month. It was an exhilarating experience that made me realise just how powerful the human mind and Spirit is!

YOU have the ability to achieve anything you put your mind too!

To change your current reality, you must really want to change and be willing to do whatever it takes. Have a think about what you want to achieve during this cleanse. Dream big and let your imagination run wild! Once you commit to your goals and dedicate yourself to this process, your life will transform in incredible ways!

My Story...

After enduring a serious injury in 2004 where I fractured L2 and L3 in my lower back, I was left bed bound for months and in chronic pain for over 7 years. 2 years after the accident at the age of 23, I was diagnosed with osteoarthritis of the spine and was suffering severely. The doctors and spine specialists told me I would be in pain for the rest of my life and I should learn to deal with it. In that moment I realised my soul purpose was to find the natural remedy for my back pain. This was the catalyst that began my life-long study into yoga, nutritional therapy, metaphysics and energy healing.

As a professional sports therapist, I had spent over a decade helping people to heal from their injuries and overcome pain and suffering. I realised it was about time to stop putting my pain to the back of my mind, pretending it was just going to disappear. It was time to take action and treat myself the same way I would treat a patient coming to see me with back pain.

On the realisation that everything easing my pain was yoga related, I created a six-week yoga therapy programme that consisted of a daily morning yoga practice, a nutritious diet plan with plenty of natural healing foods to encourage the body to repair itself, alongside working with the power of the mind and meditation.

I started this programme on the 1st January 2011 (11:11) unaware at the time it was a call from the Angels! 11:11 is the Divine Angelic Gateway to Heaven on Earth. I definitely felt a higher power was guiding me along this new journey. 2011 was the year I started listening to the voice within and uncovering my gifts and true power.

This was the big turning point in my life.
I was about to realise that miracles do exist.

I healed my chronic back pain and shifted my consciousness into realms I never knew existed.

By committing to the same yoga sequence every morning and working on my mind-set and intentions, I created the right environment for my body to heal. After just one week, I felt amazing!

It was the first time in 7 years I had gone a whole week without pain. This really motivated me to continue with the daily practice, and by the end of the 6 weeks I was ecstatic doing the happy pain-free dance! I really couldn't believe that I had done it!

It was a miracle, the pain disappeared as if by magic!

This goes to show how our expectations have the power to transform our current beliefs. I knew yoga was helping to reduce the pain and I had previously experienced pain-free days when practicing yoga, therefore my mind expected to have no pain whenever I introduced yoga into my day.

Starting my day with yoga allowed me to get into a pain-free space where my positive expectations changed the neural pathways in my brain to restructure my belief system and change the story going on between my body and brain. My thoughts and beliefs were supporting the yoga practice and creating a new positive environment inside my body and mind so that I could experience the reality I was now telling myself existed. My pain disappeared because I expected it to.

Being consistent with a regular yoga routine also balanced my mind and emotions, making me feel more whole. Before embarking on this programme, I had suffered with insomnia and depression since being a little girl. Both of these complaints naturally disappeared once I got into the routine of practicing yoga every morning and I now rarely have sleepless nights.

Understanding the dynamics of energy made me realise that the depression I suffered with growing up was actually the energy and emotions of other people. I absorbed the energies within my field and took them on as my own.

I have always been highly sensitive, and before discovering chakras and energy healing, I was on a continual rollercoaster with my emotions, always fluctuating between extreme highs and lows. Because my family are happy, outgoing and full of life, people used to tell me I had nothing to be depressed about, but they knew nothing. I suffered immensely as a child, there were dark demonic forces trying to control me and take over my life. Whenever I would tell my parents or others about my terrifying experiences, they would say it wasn't real and was all in my imagination. But it was very real for me, and it made me feel very much alone in the world as I had no one to talk to about what I was going through.

I suffered a lot through illness as a child; my throat was always swollen and sore, and at the age of 11 my tonsils were removed. Even after they was removed, I still experienced a lot of pain and swelling of the throat for my entire life, until I realised ***why*** I constantly had problems in this area.

The throat chakra is about authentic expression and communication. I have the gift of seeing into other worlds, and because I didn't understand how to use that gift, I suppressed it for many years. I wasn't speaking my truth so my throat chakra became blocked, and as a result I suffered with physical ailments and illness manifesting.

Once I started speaking my truth and honouring my gifts, my throat chakra cleared, and amazingly, all illness subsided completely. As I began to open up energetically, my awareness of the connection between everything and everyone also expanded.

After this magical healing, I knew something big was about to shift in my life, so I pressed pause on my health and fitness business, and moved over to Crete for a few months, soul searching. I soon realised that my life purpose was to share the gift of yoga after teaching yoga for free by the poolside every morning. Upon arriving back home in Manchester, I put together a new business plan, set up Ayurvedic Yoga Lifestyle in October 2011, and have dedicated my life to yoga, empowering people to transform their lives in the same way I have.

Seeking a New Calling in India

After my miraculous healing experience, I felt drawn to go to India to discover more about yoga as a therapy. My friend recommended the Yoga Vidya Gurukul ashram that he had been to; instantly I knew it was the one for me. Yogacharya Dr. Vishwas Mandlik, also known as Guruji, is the founder of the ashram. He is considered one of the foremost yoga teachers in India. Yoga Vidya Gurukul ashram is a non-profit organisation inspired and guided by the vision of Swami Satyananda of Bihar School of Yoga. I enrolled on the Yoga Therapy course and stayed at the ashram for a month during February 2012. It was a life changing experience that awakened me to a whole new dimension of existence. During my time in the ashram, my subtle vibrations changed as I opened up to a higher cosmic energy, tapping into the infinite field of pure consciousness. The whole experience was deeply awakening; I could feel my Spirit expanding from within, connecting to the Source of all creation.

My Kundalini Awakening

One day whilst sat in a lecture, I saw a radiant glow emanating around Guruji's head. I felt myself shifting into an altered state as my kundalini started pulsating at the base of my spine. Mulabandha was spontaneously contracting creating orgasmic feelings around my perineum and sex organs. Waves of euphoric energy flooded my consciousness as the energy surged all the way up my spine. A luminous light exploded out through the crown of my head and enveloped my body. My whole being, bathed in shimmering light, was vibrating at such a high frequency, it was like each of my cells internally exploded into trillions of stars making up the galaxies.

I no longer existed as a physical being my whole consciousness expanded into a state of Oneness. I was in pure ecstatic bliss!

The purpose of my trip to India was to study yoga therapy and learn how to integrate yoga into my healing programmes for patients. I had never imagined that I would return a new person.

I felt so much more sensitive to food, people, situations, places, etc. and noticed an immense rise in my spiritual energy. I love ashram life! It feels like my home. I go back often and have obtained a lot of yogic training during my stay at the ashram, including; yoga therapy, yoga psychology, kids yoga, prenatal and postnatal yoga and chakra immersion studies.

History of Yoga

Yoga dates back over 5,000 years and was first mentioned in one of the oldest sacred texts, the Rig Veda. It was first developed by the Indus–Sarasvati civilisation in Northern India. The Vedas are a collection of songs, mantras and rituals that the Brahmans and Vedic priests used. The Brahmans and Rishis developed their practices over time and documented them in a book they called The Upanishads which contains over 200 scriptures. The Bhagavad Gita, one of the most renowned of the scriptures, was composed around 500 BC.

Patanjali's yoga sutras were the first systematic presentation of yoga which he devised into 8 limbs that lead to liberation and enlightenment. Patanjali's yoga sutras date back to the second century and influence most styles of yoga today.

A few centuries after Patanjali, yoga masters developed tantra yoga, a system that consisted of radical cleansing techniques to cleanse the body and mind and break the bond to our physical existence. This led to what is now known as hatha yoga.

Yoga masters from India began to travel to the West in the late 1800's and early 1900's. Two of the most influential masters were Swami Vivekananda and Paramahansa Yogananda.

Swami Vivekananda, born January 12, 1863 in Calcutta, was the first to come over in 1893. He soon attracted followers with his lectures on spirituality and universality, and started a movement for people wanting to learn more about these vast subjects. He died on July 4, 1902 while meditating, fulfilling his prophecy that he would not live to 40 years. The cause of death was a ruptured blood vessel in his brain, which his disciples believed was due to his brahmarandhra being pierced when he attained mahasamadhi.

Paramahansa Yogananda, born January 5, 1893 in Gorakhpur, was sent by his lineage to bring the teachings of yoga to the West. Yogananda's strong influence in America led him to be considered as "The Father of Yoga in the West". His best-selling book, "Autobiography of a Yogi" describes Yogananda's search for enlightenment and is a truly inspiring read. Before departing his body, he spoke his final words recited from his poem *My India;*

"Where Ganges, woods, Himalayan caves, and men dream God—
I am hallowed; my body touched that sod."

He gazed to his third eye and his body fell to the floor. Yogananda died March 7, 1952. The medical cause of death was reported as heart failure, just like all spiritual masters, it is believed that he entered mahasamadhi.

Hatha yoga was strongly promoted in India in the 1920's and 1930's by T. Krishnamacharya, Swami Sivananda and other great yogis.

Yoga has developed greatly over the past decade and there are so many unique styles available to choose from.

The Chakra Yoga Cleanse is based upon traditional Hatha Yoga, with an emphasis on the chakras, and infused with many alternative therapies that can assist you on your journey.

Benefits of Yoga

Yoga opens up energetic pathways in the body, assisting us to release blockages and get the energy moving freely to improve health and the functioning of bodily systems. It helps us to break free from any unhealthy boundaries that we may have created physically, mentally, emotionally, energetically or spiritually.

Once you commit to a regular yoga practice, you will feel more energised, stronger, fitter, healthier and happier, with increased confidence and self-esteem. You learn to listen to your body and become more in touch with yourself and the messages being communicated from your body to your mind.

Yoga improves your overall sense of wellbeing. This lifestyle raises your consciousness, perceptions, and quality of life.

The benefits truly are limitless. By using the power of intention, we add direction and focus to our practice to help us achieve our goals on and off the mat. These intentions can be used consistently throughout the day as affirmations to help you achieve your goals more quickly.

Just like most people, I began my yoga practice to become more flexible and to calm my overactive mind. Somewhere along the wonderful journey of discovering yoga, I realised there is so much more to this incredible ancient practice than the physical and mental benefits. We open up energetically and start to feel things in our subtle environment that are not recognised by the human eye; we awaken to the Spirit realm and are more sensitive to other dimensions. This spiritual awakening transforms our lives and inspires us to a new way of living. Our increased sensitivity to data within our energy field fine tunes our intuition so we can receive and interpret the energetic messages being delivered to us.

This inner resource is a gift and a mystical skill that can be developed through yoga; it is our cosmic navigation system

Our natural state is health and our body will always try to guide us back into alignment with the natural world. The body resonates with the law of nature, it is designed to be harmonious with the environment. When we listen to that inner voice, we maintain health and harmony within.

The Importance of a Daily Practice

A daily spiritual practice (sadhana) restores balance in your body, mind, heart and Spirit. By establishing a regular routine where you start your day with yoga, you will feel healthier, happier and more positive throughout the day. Your sadhana will empower you to commit to your intention and keep you focused towards achieving your goals for the day.

A daily practice has positive effects on all the systems of the body. Starting your day with yoga raises your vibrations, improves physical health and boosts positive mental energy. You will feel stronger physically, mentally, emotionally and spiritually.

Pranayama (breath work) is an integral part of your yoga practice and should be practiced every day during yoga, and also independently throughout the day any time you feel yourself struggling with the daily stresses and strains of life. Always make sure you are relaxed when practicing pranayama, there should be no tension or strain. Breathe with awareness through the nose. Always begin with basic abdominal breathing to fully utilise the breath and to prepare for more advanced techniques.

Patanjali's 8 Limbs of Yoga

There is more to yoga than just the physical postures. Patanjali encapsulated the yoga scriptures/sutras and developed the 8 limbs of yoga to guide us on our journey to liberation, inner peace and self-realisation. The 8 limbs of yoga can be seen as a tree.

Patanjali's yoga sutras are the most prevalent ancient spiritual texts for the practice of yoga. The 8 limbs act as a guideline on how to live a meaningful and purposeful life. They teach us how to integrate yoga into our lives to bring balance to body, mind, heart and Spirit.

Pantanjali was a man of great wisdom who was the founder and father of yoga. He was considered to be a fully self-realised avatar, who had mastered the mind, the body, the senses, and even this physical world. He was also a profound master of knowledge; which made him an amazing philosopher and teacher of how to master your life.

We can eliminate all of our negative conditionings that are lodged within our body and mind and create the foundations for a healthy balanced life by applying the eightfold path approach of classical yoga.

The 8 limbs of yoga are:

- Yama
- Niyama
- Asana
- Pranayama
- Pratyahara
- Dharana
- Dhyana
- Samadhi

The yamas and niyamas create the ethical foundations of human life for us to follow so we grow and evolve spiritually. In yoga this is known as dharma, 'the correct way of living'. Following the principles of yamas and niyamas brings balance into our lives and provides overall health and wellbeing. It helps us to focus our mind and actions so we live congruent to the laws of nature.

The 5 Yamas – Social Disciplines

Yamas are ethical, moral and societal standards for us to live by to bring balance to our outer nature and social interactions in the world. They include our behaviour and how we conduct ourselves.

***SIMPLE LIFE* – Aparigraha** relates to non-attachment and living a simple life. Non-attachment requires letting go of the need to own things. Life is so much more than the material possessions we have, and the practice of aparigraha helps us to realise this. Living a simple minimal life liberates us, freeing us from the material world. Everything you think you own actually owns you. Try letting go of things you don't really need. Give away clothes you haven't worn for a while, clear out your cupboards and draws, and notice how light and different you feel afterwards. It is beneficial to clear out the kitchen cupboards before embarking on your cleanse.

This yama teaches us to not be greedy; to be happy and grateful for what we have got. Aparigraha also teaches us to let go of all attachments to the outcome of our actions. Do your work whole-heartedly and don't worry about what will come of it. When we detach from the fruits of our actions, we are practicing aparigraha, living selflessly.

Everything in life passes; nothing lasts. Practice non-attachment to your thoughts and emotions, simply let them be. We cannot change the past, it has already happened, and we do not know what will happen in the future; it hasn't happened yet. Be conscious of your mind in the present, a silent observer of your thoughts. Let go of all attachments to thoughts and feelings and set your mind free.

***SELF CONTROL* – Brahmacharya** relates to the focus of our energy. Working on yourself requires discipline and self-control. To use our energy in the right way we must learn to listen to our body. Always think about where you are directing your energy, is it helpful or harmful? By choosing to focus our energy on positive thoughts throughout the day, we are directing our energy in the correct way. Once we become aware of how our body responds in different situations, we can focus our energies on cultivating the most wholesome and vibrant lifestyle that best serves us.

This yama also relates to disciplining and preserving the use of sexual energy. The self-control, as promoted by Brahmacharya, increases life force energy, develops strength in body and mind, boosts creativity, and progresses you on your spiritual path.

Sexual energy resides in the sacral chakra. This powerful creative life force energy can be transmuted into the higher chakras and channelled towards what you want to achieve in your life i.e. devotion to God, meditation or your craft. Channelling this energy towards your desired outcome will speed up the manifestation of your goals. As you move the energy into manipura, your centre of willpower and transformation, you raise your level of awareness and mental power.

Sexual transmutation is the 'Magic of Alchemy'

Focusing on your goals and transmuting your sexual energy into the higher centres moves you beyond sexual gratification and into the empowering state of self-control and self-mastery.

HONESTY - Atesya relates to honesty and non-stealing. Do not take property that belongs to others. Asteya relates to truthfulness, being content with what you have and living an honest life. This includes not stealing or manipulating other people's energy to make yourself feel better or for personal gain.

We can also relate this to time, and allow ourselves to slow down and really enjoy what we are doing with conscious intention, instead of rushing onto the next thing on our to-do list.

We should live completely in the present moment. Whenever we are not in the present moment, we are stealing from ourselves the experience of being alive right now, enjoying what life has to offer. Train yourself to live fully in the present moment; be kind, honest and loving to yourself.

***KINDNESS* - Ahimsa** relates to loving kindness and non-violence. This yama teaches us to be kind to everyone, including ourselves. Ahimsa is the absence of violence from your body, mind and soul. It includes thoughts towards oneself as well as others. We must never wish harm onto others, as this attracts negative thoughts and violence in the mind. When you think harmful thoughts, negative energy builds up in the brain and neural pathways arc created that can lead to harmful words and actions. Our thoughts are so powerful, they transform the brain on a neurological level. Replace any harmful thoughts with positive mantras to create healthy and positive neural pathways. Mantras are a powerful way to change our thought-form vibrations and restore balance to our mind, body and soul.

To love and to be loved is life's greatest gift

Embrace love in all that you do and be compassionate to your fellow human beings and Mother Earth. Following a vegetarian diet shows compassion to animals and all living beings. Practicing non-violence is the most important thing we can do to create a healthy relationship with the world. Ahimsa develops compassion in our hearts for all of humanity and raises our vibrations preventing us from picking up on negative energy.

***TRUTH* - Satya** relates to being truthful in one's thoughts, words and actions, becoming One with our true nature. The practice of Satya means carefully considering our words so they are aligned with loving kindness, ahimsa. According to Patanjali, words can only reflect truth when they flow from the Spirit of non-violence. Being untruthful distorts the mind and affects our actions. Speaking from your heart with love and compassion reflects satya in your life for yourself and others. Stand up for what you believe in and speak your truth with authenticity and love.

Harmony in both body and mind comes from us leading honest, truthful and detached lives. When we do not follow the right social conducts for living, we become out of balance energetically and disease manifests in our body, mind and emotions.

The 5 Niyamas – Personal Disciplines

Niyama yoga consists of 5 internal practices that give us self-discipline and inner-strength to progress on the spiritual path to self-realisation.

***DISCIPLINE* - Tapas** relates to the heat inside us, our inner flame, passions and burning desire to better ourselves. This inner fire motivates us to grow, evolve and transform our lower energies into something more positive. It relates to us making changes to our lives and certain habits, like letting go of addictive behaviours.

Self-discipline is required so that we can direct our energy and actions towards our goal to become a better person and create a better society. We must be willing to let go of distractions and sacrifice anything that may not be congruent with our goal.

Self-discipline helps to balance the mind and 'pitta dosha'.

***CONTENTMENT* – Santosa** relates to inner peace and contentment; maintaining a peaceful and cheerful mental state. Santosa is the realisation that happiness comes from within. External happiness is short-lived and leads to addictive tendencies and behaviours. Contentment leads to inner peace and a calm happy mind. Be happy and grateful for what you have. Every morning when you wake up, begin your day with this mantra, "I am so happy and grateful..."

For example, "I am so happy and grateful to wake up with a roof over my head. I am so happy and grateful to access clean water and for the delicious food that nourishes me. I am so happy and grateful for this flavoursome herbal tea and for the plantation workers that made it possible for these tea leaves to be here for me now." Give thanks for everything in your life that you are grateful for, all the small things that you may have previously taken for granted.

Beginning your day with gratitude opens your heart to the abundance of the Universe and raises your consciousness to higher levels of peace and contentment.

***PURITY* - Sauca** relates to purity and cleanliness of the body, mind and environment. Sauca represents a clear mind, with pure thoughts and good speech. It applies to purity of body and mind, both internal and external. To cleanse the mind, we must focus on positive thoughts, emotions and impressions, and let go of the negative and impure thoughts, emotions and impressions such as those found on the TV, radio and in the news. Negative energies create disharmony and cause mental and physical problems to manifest. Following a pure vegetarian diet purifies our physical body and creates the right environment to heal and restore the tissues in our body. Yoga is the best aid for strengthening the body and mind and cleaning out the energy channels.

***SELF-STUDY* - Svadhyaya** relates to the study of Self to help us understand who we are and why we are here. Spiritual teachings open up our mind and consciousness so that we can develop a deeper understanding of the Universe and our role within it.

Svadhyaya is a continual practice that awakens our inner light and thirst for truth. We can create the life of our dreams by applying the knowledge we attain during self-study and contemplation.

Living in an ashram or monastery with an advanced teacher or a saintly being develops svadhyaya quickly. You can create your own spiritual sanctuary within the comfort of your home and use the practices in this book to develop your personal sadhana and enhance your lifestyle.

This niyama also relates to us honouring our elders and the contribution they have made to society.

Self-study helps to balance prana and 'vata dosha'.

***SURRENDER* - Isvara pranidhana** teaches us to surrender and trust in life. We are all Divine beings. Isvara relates to us being One with the whole of creation and recognising the Divine in everyone and everything. Being open to this omnipresent energy protects us from negativity and keeps us in high vibrations connected to the Source of all creation.

Devotion balances 'kapha dosha' leading us ultimately to Samadhi.

Asana: The Physical Postures

The physical postures have so many amazing health benefits for physical, mental, emotional and spiritual wellbeing, including increased flexibility, improved muscle tone and posture, elevated energy levels, and a reduction in stress, anxiety and depression. Asanas boost circulation and oxygenation, improving nutrient supply into the bloodstream and organs to nourish the physical body and the mind. Physical postures open the body energetically so we can heal on a deep cellular level. Asanas also develop the habit of discipline and the ability to concentrate; preparing the body for meditation. Regular practice of yoga improves quality of life and helps us to master the mind and attain samadhi.

Pranayama: Control of Life Force

Prana is the invisible life force that creates movement of all things in creation. Energies flow from the chakras along energy channels also known as nadis. We have 72,000 nadis in our bodies which transport prana (life force) to every single organism in our being. The 3 main nadis are ida (lunar, feminine energy), pingala (solar, masculine energy) and sushumna (central channel). These energies move up and down the spinal column balancing and energising each of the chakras.

Ida governs the right brain and left side of the body, connecting us with the cool, calm, loving and compassionate energies of our Divine nature. Pingala governs the left brain and right side of the body, connecting us with the hot, dynamic, proactive and driven aspects of our Divine nature. Sushumna is the peaceful space between these 2 energies that brings us the tremendous healing potential of being in the present moment.

When our prana is high, we have a stronger resistance to illness and are able to eliminate toxins and heal more efficiently. When our nadis become blocked, disease manifests in the body. The most effective way of purifying the nadis is by practicing pranayama.

Pranayama raises our vibrations and energy levels, and balances both hemispheres of the brain to initiate healing and higher states of consciousness.

For the average individual, there are areas of consciousness that remain in darkness. By awakening to higher states and becoming aware of pranic energy, we illuminate these dark areas by bringing light and space into the body and mind. This kind of awareness opens us up to a new dimension of existence where we can tap into the healing potential of our Divine Self and Spirit.

Lower vibrational thoughts and feelings use maximum prana and leave us feeling depleted and exhausted, which leads to anxiety, stress and depression. Practicing pranayama charges the prana and increases our vibrations, giving us an abundance of energy and increasing our healing potential. Our thoughts and intentions become empowered so we can achieve our desired outcome.

By bringing awareness to the breath and paying attention to the inhalation and exhalation, we can calm the body and mind, relaxing all of our systems and bring about positive shifts in our health.

Breath awareness is very effective for reducing pain and stress, and aiding muscle relaxation.

energy levels. It enables us to recognise the connection between the breath, mind and emotions.

The first 4 limbs of yoga refine our personality and allow us to gain mastery over the body, preparing us for the second half of the yoga journey which deals with transcending the mind and senses to attain a higher state of consciousness.

Pratyahara: Withdrawal of the Senses

"Just as a tortoise withdraws its limbs, so when a man withdraws his senses from the sense objects, his wisdom becomes steady." Bhagavad Gita

Pratyahara relates to cultivating detachment from our senses and external stimuli. We are constantly bombarded with sensory overload and are often distracted by sensory pleasures and habits.

The practice of pratyahara gives us the opportunity to step back and look at ourselves, observing cravings and habits that can interfere with our inner growth. It helps us to break negative habits and thought patterns, reducing our desire to fulfil sensory pleasures. When we withdraw the senses, our intuitive mind awakens.

Pratyahara is a bridge between the external aspects of yoga (the first 4 limbs) and internal aspects of yoga (the final 3 limbs). This limb applies to internalising the consciousness so that the senses do not reach their respective centres in the brain. This practice offers us the haven of silence and a profound state of relaxation. Our self-awareness expands as we direct our attention inwards.

The last 3 limbs of patanjali's yoga sutras, known as 'sanyama' (mastery), should be considered together, there is no separation between these final 3 stages of the 8 limbed path, they all merge together as one.

Dharana: Fixed Concentration

Dharana relates to concentrating on a single object or mantra, focusing all of your attention on a single point for extended periods of time to deal with the distractions of the mind. Dharana teaches us to control the mind by channelling all our thought power in one direction. We can make a decision to change, and then apply conscious effort into realising it.

During dharana practice, if the mind wanders off, we must bring it back to the experience of concentrating on your dristi (fixed focal point). For example, you can focus awareness on your breath, or use a candle flame as focal point. Once you can fix your concentration without any distractions, you are in the stage of dharana and will experience peace of mind and contentment. The more you practice, the longer the state of dharana lasts for.

In everyday life, we can see dharana active whenever a person is fully present and focused completely on what they are doing. For instance, when you are absorbed in an activity and immersed in what you are doing, your mind is clear and you are living in the moment. A fine example of this is witnessing an artist completely absorbed in painting and seeming almost at one with his artwork, or an athlete who immerses himself so fully into his sport as if nothing else exists; he is fully in the zone. When a child is totally absorbed in play they appear to be in a different world, nothing else matters to them other than that moment of play; they are fully in dharana. We can learn so much from observing children. They bring us back into the moment and open our hearts to the magical awe-inspiring wonders of life.

When you are consumed by too many thoughts, inner conflicts arise, creating disharmony in the mind-body connection which leads to mental distress and potential illness. Dharana calms and focuses the mind which leads to an inner peace and a happier attitude towards life. My favourite way of practising dharana is to watch the sheer magnificence of sunrises and sunsets, absorbing myself completely in the beauty of the sun, the giver of life.

Dhyana: Meditation

Dhyana is the unbroken and uninterrupted experience of concentration. The mind is still, with no thoughts at all. It takes a lot of strength and stamina to reach this state of stillness. Dhyana is a deeper stage of dharana that induces a state of tranquillity throughout our whole being. We attain a heightened level of awareness and move into a higher state of consciousness.

Meditation is extremely powerful and a great way to relax and revitalise the whole being; body, mind, heart and spirit, enhancing energy, strength and vitality. It helps us to control our mind and provides a great opportunity for us to be self-aware in our actions and during difficult situations. It teaches us to be more present in our lives so we can be more mindful in our interactions.

Dhyana is a wonderful tool that can help us understand our inner world and the workings of our minds. Our attention is generally external and we are constantly bombarded with impressions from the world around us and other peoples' opinions. Meditation helps us to cultivate self-awareness so that we can observe our inner world, our feelings, emotions, reactions, responses and expectations. This awareness allows us to learn how to control our thoughts and respond to situations instead of reacting to them.

Regular practice of meditation calms the mind and central nervous system, reducing anxiety, stress and depression. Serotonin levels increase, influencing mood and behaviour which helps to control thoughts, focus the mind and increase creativity. Spiritually, you will find peace of mind, forgiveness, compassion, self-realisation, wisdom, enlightenment and a deeper understanding of yourself and others. You will notice an increase in the synchronicities in your life and magic will appear in unexpected ways. Your attitude towards life will change as you become an embodiment of light.

Just 2 x 10 minutes meditation practices a day will make a huge difference in your productivity and will leave you feeling inspired with an abundance of energy to get things done without even thinking about it. Your mind will become so focused on achieving your goals that you may even get more done than you anticipated and feel more confident and at peace as a result.

Always be conscious of your actions, along with your thoughts and feelings; they shape your future. During the day, be mindful of your actions and reflect on your choices. Ask yourself if your choice will bring you closer or further away from your goal or desired outcome. Once you become aware of your thoughts and feelings you can transform your life in so many ways.

In dharana, we concentrate on an object; in dhyana, we become the object and the object becomes us. The object disappears, we disappear and all becomes One. If you are focusing on a mantra, you become One with it. In this deep profound state of meditation, there are no borders or boundaries; we become One with the Universe and the whole of creation.

Samadhi: Enlightenment

Samadhi is our natural state

We are One. We are Divine. We are Sacred.

In samadhi, the object which you were meditating upon becomes pure essence. Dharana and dhyana merge together and become One. Everything is formless, just pure consciousness. You come back to your natural state of purity and illumination.

We attain Samadhi when we transcend the body, mind and emotions, moving beyond ordinary reality into a higher state of consciousness.

We become One with life itself and realise the infinite Universe that resides within us. The Divine cosmic energy flows through our vessel and illuminates us from the core of our existence. The remembrance of our Divine essence brings us into a state of eternal bliss, samadhi.

Chapter 2: The Subtle Energy Body

Energy, Vibration & Frequency

"Everything is energy and that is all there is to it. Match the frequency of the reality you want and you cannot help but get that reality. It can be no other way. This is not philosophy, this is physics."
Albert Einstein

Energy is the source of our vitality and the building blocks of all matter. Everything in the entire Universe is energy vibrating at different frequencies. Energy varies from solid material objects that vibrate slowly and appear dense, to electromagnetic energy which vibrates so fast we cannot see it with the human eye. If we were to look at a single atom under a microscope, we would notice that space occupies the majority of the atom. When atoms join together to create physical objects, they appear to be very solid and dense, but in reality, everything tangible in this Universe can be broken down to a single atom that predominantly consists of nothing but space vibrating and interacting with its environment. Once we realise that everything is energy, our perceptions change and we have the potential to completely transform our lives.

The Human Energy System

You are a multidimensional electromagnetic being

The body is made up of inter-dependent energy systems. When these systems are balanced and aligned, they maintain our health and wellbeing.

An electromagnetic energy field, also known as our aura, or toroidal energy field, surrounds and protects our physical body. We interact with the world energetically and our auras are constantly changing depending on our surroundings.

Everything in creation has a toroidal energy field (aura) surrounding it: people, plants, trees, planets, absolutely everything.

Right in the centre of every toroidal energy field there is a "zero point" sphere, which is the ultimate space of pure potential where nothing and everything exists. This is the central point of our manifestation.

Every toroidal has 2 holes, one black negatively-charged hole that sucks energy in, and one white positively-charged hole that emits energy. The energy of the torus continually flows out and back into itself; it is constantly refreshing itself with new life force.

The body is a self-sustained electromagnetic field of consciousness, intimately connected to the quantum field

The axis of the heart torus extends from the base of the spine to the crown of the head. The energy and consciousness flows in through the crown chakra, circulates through the whole chakra system, and then exits through the root chakra into the Earth and physical realm. This flow of energy is known as the manifestation current. When the energy system is blocked, the life force leaks out of the body, leaving us feeling depleted and lacking in energy. Our aim is to tune into the energy field and regain mastery over our senses to bring equilibrium back into the system.

We each vibrate at different frequencies depending on how we think and feel. As we vibrate, we attract what is similar to us. The Law of Attraction affirms that like attracts like; whatever you think about you attract into your energy field. Every thought you have is shaping your reality. As soon as you change your beliefs, you allow your cells, genes and DNA to upgrade to a higher level of consciousness altering your state of reality in which the world around you will also change. The outer world is a reflection of your inner world. The more peace you embody within you, the more peace you feel in the world.

Be mindful of what goes into your body and consciousness

Everything you put into your body has an energetic frequency. It is important that you are aware of the quality of energy that goes into the body to maintain high vibrations and good health. This includes thoughts, impressions, social media, television, music, food, and the people we choose to spend time with.

Lower thoughts and feelings such as fear, anger, resentment, guilt and shame all lower your vibrations and attract negative experiences into your life. Love vibrates at 528 hertz and allows the body, mind and spirit to heal itself naturally. Anything above love is considered peace, bliss, higher consciousness, ecstasy.

We create our realities with the thoughts that we send out into the world; we can change our story at any moment

Becoming aware of your energetic body gives you the power to feel energies that are entering into your field. This awareness enables you to cut off negative energy immediately so that it doesn't penetrate deeper levels of your being. When you are not consciously aware at this level, the energetic disturbance penetrates your physical body and you may feel uneasy, sick or other unsettling feelings for no apparent reason.

When you do not act on the early signs of disease becoming present in the body, it develops further, causing discomfort, pain and illness. The longer you leave a complaint, the longer it takes to heal. If you affirm to yourself once you get ill that something is out of balance energetically and you allow the Divine light to enter your consciousness to heal and bring balance back into your system, you will soon be well. You will hear the Divine guidance from your higher Self, directing you to make correct choices in your lifestyle to seek balance and harmony with nature, which will result in good health. There is no place for illness in the body or mind when you are vibrating at your highest potential, only love and light exists at this level of consciousness.

Any pain or suffering we endure is there to guide us back into alignment. When we take time to listen to the body, and follow the guidance we receive, pain naturally diminishes. We all have the potential to recharge our energy levels and maintain equilibrium and great health. The key is to learn how to tap into universal energy, the source of all Creation, and keep that connection to the Divine flowing freely and abundantly.

Chakras & Nadis

We have 7 main energy centres (chakras) in the body situated along the spine. The chakras are associated with the rainbow colours and each one holds a different vibration and frequency.

Chakras are multi-dimensional gateways that allow us to access different states of consciousness, they also govern different aspects of our health and wellbeing.

Each chakra has lower and higher aspects. Our life lessons reside in the lower aspects of each chakra. This includes illusions, pain and suffering. Our life lessons repeat themselves until we learn from them and change the way we respond to any given event. Once we break this karmic cycle, we move away from illusions and suffering towards liberation, freedom and happiness. As we become aware of our higher Self we move into the higher aspect of each chakra.

We have many minor chakras that assist our major chakras. They are situated parallel on both sides of the body to maintain balance and alignment of the system as a whole.

The chakras emanate electromagnetic energy into our auras, creating sheaths, also known as koshas, around our physical body. These sheaths make up our aura, which extends roughly 20 feet around the body, attracting that which we vibrate. The aura processes and exchanges energy within our field.

Each of the petals that are found on the chakras represents the nadis (energetic pathways) that distribute that chakra's energy around the body to the specific organs and glands.

Anatomy & Physiology of Chakras

Each chakra is associated with an endocrine gland and group of nerves, also known as a nerve plexus; a cluster of neurotransmitter receptors that exchange communication between the mind and body. Each chakra also governs certain areas of the body and bridge the dimensions of consciousness.

The Nervous System

The nervous system consists of the Central Nervous System (CNS) and Peripheral Nervous System (PNS). The central nervous system is the primary control centre for communication between the body and mind; it is made up of the brain and spinal cord.

The peripheral nervous system consists of nerve fibres that connect the central nervous system to the limbs, organs and skin. It consists of 12 pairs of cranial nerves which radiate out from the brain to all areas of the face and neck; and 31 pairs of spinal nerves which radiate out from the spine to rest of the body.

The peripheral nerves transmit voluntary and involuntary actions. This system comprises of 2 sub-divisions, the Autonomic Nervous System (ANS) and the Somatic Nervous System (SNS).

The autonomic nervous system connects the central nervous system to the organs of the body. It controls and regulates involuntary bodily functions such as breathing, digestive processes, urination, sexual arousal, blood flow and heartbeat. It is the master regulator of metabolism, directly controlling energy utilisation and keeps us alive without conscious thought. It has 2 opposing branches; the sympathetic (fight, flight or freeze) and parasympathetic (rest and digest) nervous systems.

The somatic nervous system carries sensory and motor information to and from the central nervous system via sensory (afferent) and motor (efferent) neurons. The sensory neurons carry information from sensory organs to the central nervous system. They are found in the skin, ears, eyes, nose and tongue. The motor neurons carry information away from the brain and spinal cord to the effector organs, glands and tissues, enabling their functioning.

The Endocrine System

The endocrine system governs physical wellbeing and is responsible for every cell, organ and function in the body. The endocrine glands regulate bodily functions by secreting hormones throughout the body.

The hypothalamus connects the endocrine system to the nervous system, it instructs the pituitary gland to start or stop making hormones. The endocrine glands are, pituitary, pineal, thyroid, parathyroid, thymus, pancreas, ovaries and testes and adrenals.

Sound helps to balance and regulate the endocrine system.

Psychology of the Chakras

You are already enlightened,
It is your natural state of being

It is no secret you are an enlightened being, but the veil of illusion covering the third eye chakra prevents you from seeing this reality. The trap of the mind and ego keeps us identified with the personality and our roles in life.

Transcend lower levels of awareness
to reach your full potential

To evolve through the chakras, we can look at different personality aspects and how they relate to the gunas.

Gunas are the subtle energies of everything in nature, they make up the mind and body. Each of your chakras function at different levels of consciousness and represent one or more of the gunas; tamas, rajas and sattva.

Tamas is the lowest energy and represents inertia and darkness. Tamasic personalities are low in energy and have no enthusiasm for life.

As we evolve through the states of consciousness within the chakras, there are in between stages. From tamas a person moves into tamasic-rajasic, where they have little motivation but are still stuck in the darker energies. When their motivation improves, their rajasic qualities increase and they shift into rajasic-tamasic. This is a person who has realised their power, yet still exhibits destructive behaviours. Once the tamasic energies are pacified, the person moves into rajasic.

Rajasic personalities are ambitious, ego-centrical and driven by personal gain. With a lot of fire, they can tend to over-indulge in life's pleasures, and they seek happiness from outside of themselves. As a person further develops their consciousness, they move into rajasic-sattvic and towards a more balanced and peaceful life. At this level of awareness, consideration for others is developed, and it becomes less about what they can get out of a situation and more geared towards how they can help others. Once compassion for others transcends their desires for personal gain, this person transcends into sattva-rajas, where the ego is overshadowed by sattva. This person realises that happiness is an inside job.

Sattvic personalities are calm, peaceful and live in harmony with nature. They have attained inner happiness and contentment, and are fully in the flow. They are a channel of Divine grace, radiating peace, love and light into the world. Their presence lights up a room.

The final stage of consciousness is enlightenment; living in a state of Oneness and bliss. The prevailing attitude of an enlightened person is one of love, compassion and joy. They are open to the mystical wonders of the Universe and channel Divine messages from the higher dimensions, communicating them to the world with clarity and wisdom.

In the diagram on the next page you can see the evolution of consciousness from a tamasic state on the left, moving through rajas in the middle, the energy of movement and action, and into sattva, the enlightened state of being.

As we learn the lessons of each chakra and work on ourselves to develop spiritually, we restore our natural sattvic nature that was always there waiting to be realised. This process enables us to shift our consciousness from the 3rd dimension reality into the 5th dimension and beyond.

The path towards self-realisation offers us many gifts, which can be experienced along the journey as we travel over the rainbow; from darkness and ignorance into light and eternal bliss.

For example, when you work on the lower aspects of swadhistana and overcome your addictive behaviours, you unlock the creativity within your sacral chakra and are gifted with an abundance of creative life force energy to manifest your unique talents in the world.

Once you have awakened the dormant life force potential within all 7 chakras, you activate your full potential and become a master of your Self and your Universe.

We will look at the personalities of each guna in relation to the chakras in the next chapter.

Somewhere Over the Rainbow

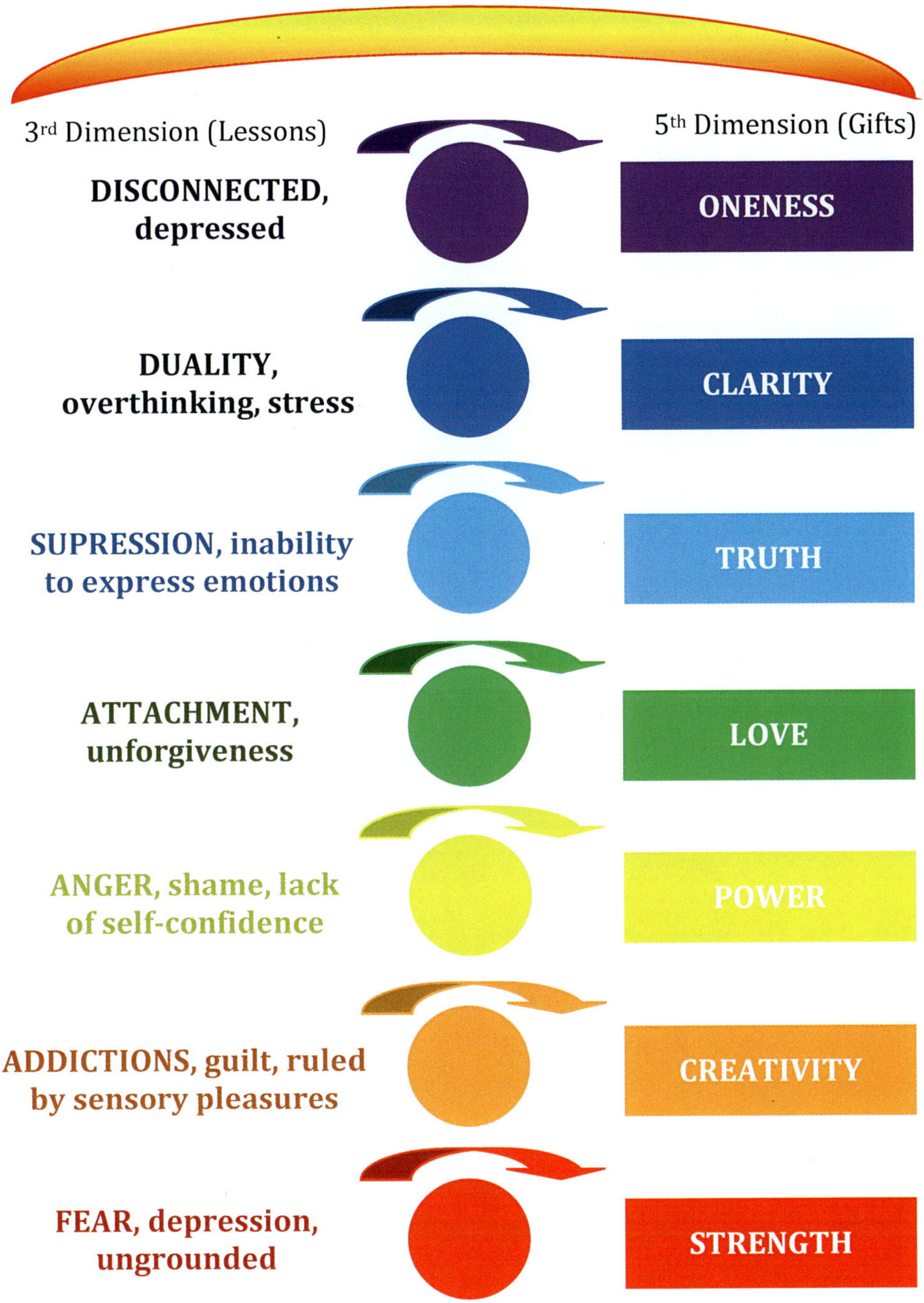

Dimensions of Consciousness

Love and fear cannot co-exist in the same place, when you focus on love, your fears disappear

For many years now, we have been transitioning from the 3rd physical dimension of living a normal ordinary life, to the 5th spiritual dimension where we are waking up to our Divine nature and realising our potential. There are 2 driving forces in this Universe and we gravitate to one more than the other. These energies are:

LOVE or FEAR

Focusing on love raises our vibrations, elevating our Spirit into the 5th dimension. All of our chakras flow in harmony with each other and we feel vibrant and full of high vibrational life force. We are open to the Spirit realm and are nourished by celestial beings guiding us on our journey.

Focusing on fear lowers our vibrations, keeping us stuck in the 3rd dimension. We become trapped in the lower aspects of each chakra and struggle to move up in the heart chakra where we have the potential to heal. You are ruled by fear, addictive behaviours and anger, consumed by lower entities that feed off your lower vibrational energy.

This can equate to positive (loved-based benevolent energy) and negative (fear-based maleficent energy). Remember, energy flows to where your attention goes. The more you focus on love, the lighter you become and the brighter you shine!

Fear is the lowest vibration and keeps us in pain and suffering. When we focus on fear, we attract more negative energy into our lives and we are stuck in a vicious cycle of pessimism and not being able to see a brighter future.

Love is a high vibration that creates healing within ourselves and also emanates out into our surroundings to heal others and Mother Earth. Love is the most nourishing form of prana there is.

Once we achieve inner love for ourselves and naturally send that out into the world we live in, we tap into universal love and unity consciousness.

We must rise above the need to obtain our energy solely from external sources, especially that from other people. This only creates addictive behaviours and the need to always search outside of ourselves for something more. The spark of love you have for yourself, awakens you to who you truly are; a multi-dimensional being of love and light.

The 3rd Dimension - Duality Consciousness

We are spiritual beings having a human experience, living on a planet that is governed by polar opposites

There are 2 aspects to everything in creation, and both are necessary for us to experience life on Earth. You cannot have one without the other, they are 2 sides of the same coin. Light/dark, up/down, left/right, night/day, sun/moon, love/fear, happy/sad, good/bad, etc. The 3rd dimension is a trap of the ego mind, an illusion that we are separate and limited in material form.

This relates to the lower aspects of the chakras, the tamasic and rajasic qualities. If you are not happy with the way things are in your life, make a conscious effort to change. By recognising that everything is energy, you have the power to control the energy within and around you. Life is a choice. You get to choose what you want to experience.

Change your vibration, Change your life!

We have 2 choices, we can either ***choose*** to emit a certain frequency and radiate our light out into the world to make positive change, or we can become victim to the energies in our environment and be controlled by external circumstances.

We live in a society that promotes the latter, and it is our job to peel back those layers of conditioning and re-connect to the light that shines from within; our true nature.

The 5th Dimension - Beyond Ordinary Reality

You are a multi-dimensional sovereign being,
Awaken to your inner divinity and set yourself free!

We are all One, connected by our DNA through the electromagnetic energy fields of our light bodies. Once we shift our awareness to higher states of consciousness, the illusion falls away and we experience a deeper and more meaningful relationship with our Divine nature. We naturally embody 5th dimension consciousness by fully stepping into our power as sovereign beings.

Chapter 3:

Journey Through the Rainbow Bridge

Within our first energy centre, the root chakra, we have an unlimited supply of dormant energies ready to be awakened

This dormant energy is also known as kundalini or Shakti, the feminine principle, Mother Earth. Awakening the kundalini energy at the base of the spine at muladhara is the beginning of our spiritual journey. Our aim is to raise the kundalini energy up through the chakras to develop awareness and consciousness to every level of our existence. The 3 main nadis; ida, pingala and sushumna begin their journey at the base of the spine at muladhara.

As you journey up through the chakras, these multi-dimensional gateways will allow you to access different states of consciousness, uncovering your true potential and eternal Self.

The energy of pure consciousness that exists at the crown chakra is represented by Shiva, the masculine principle that leads us to liberation. This chakra has the highest and most subtle vibration.

Shiva and Shakti seek to reunite with each other; their potential is designed to flow like an eternal dance moving up and down the spine passing through each of the chakras in balance, grace and harmony with each other.

Unaware of this energy, most people get stuck in the lower three chakras and are controlled by fear (lower aspects of the root chakra), anxiety and addictions (lower aspects of the sacral chakra) and anger (lower aspects of the solar plexus chakra).

The Shakti energy is unable to move any higher, therefore, physical, emotional and mental problems arise until you release these blockages and allow the energy to flow up through the chakras freely. By working on the lower aspects of each chakra you can let go of self-limiting beliefs and negative habits including thoughts, feelings and addictive behaviours. We can bring any illness back to the root cause on an energetic level, removing the blockages and balancing the flow of prana (life force).

Once you get the energy moving up into the heart chakra, you raise your vibrations to a level where you heal your body, mind and soul. This is the meeting point of our physical and spiritual Self and the bridge between Heaven and Earth.

We live in a perpetual cycle of giving and receiving, always adapting to the vibrations in our environment. If you are a sensitive person you may pick up on other people's negative energy and take it on as your own. It is important to protect yourself from picking up on harsh energies from those around you.

Most people are disconnected from their spiritual Self and as a result of this, the Shiva energy gets blocked at the crown chakra which prevents the energy from moving down towards Shakti. By opening up to universal energy and focusing the mind on channelling consciousness into the lower chakras, we are able to get the energies flowing freely towards each other to restore balance.

When the energy flows freely through each of the chakras, Shiva and Shakti finally unite at ajna, the third eye chakra. The veil of duality is lifted, exposing the truth of Oneness.

The current that moves up from muladhara (root chakra) to sahasrara (crown chakra) liberates us from the clutches of pain and we realise higher levels of consciousness and truth.

The current that moves down from sahasrara to muladhara gives us the potential to manifest our thoughts and desires here in the physical world.

Anything we can perceive in our mind we can achieve in our life

By holding a clear vision in your third eye (ajna chakra) of what you want to achieve, and creating a powerful intention around your vision, you are sending thought forms out into the Universe that begin to shape your future in positive ways. You tap into the cosmic energy of the Universe and channel it from Shiva consciousness into the crown chakra and all the way down to the base of the spine, into the roots of Mother Earth as you manifest your intentions in the physical plane of your reality.

The Dance of Shiva/Shakti

The Divine feminine and masculine principles are in everything in creation. These 2 energies manifest on all planes of existence and in their separate form, create duality. The feminine is the moon, and masculine is the sun. Hatha yoga is the pathway to unite the energies of the sun and moon to restore balance of the feminine and masculine, yin/yang energies.

Restoring Balance to the Chakras

When the chakras become blocked, overactive or underactive, this imbalance has a knock-on effect on the corresponding organs leading to illness and disease manifesting in the body and mind. By awakening each chakra, you can bring balance, positivity, peace, clarity, high energy and success into your life.

Actively working with your energetic body will empower you to balance your chakras and heal yourself on every level; physically, mentally, emotionally and spiritually.

As you awaken each of the 7 main chakras along the spine, starting at the root chakra and the physical aspects of your being, moving up through each of the chakras connecting to the element that governs each of these powerful energy centres, you begin to peel back the layers of previous conditionings and heal on a deep cellular level.

You can use many therapies to restore balance in your energy body. On the ***Chakra Yoga Cleanse*** detailed in chapter 6, these therapies include; nature, yoga, meditation, nutrition, sound, colour, crystals, aromatherapy and working with Archangels.

<u>Benefits of Spending Time in Nature</u>

Have you ever noticed how alive you feel when you're outside in nature?

Being in nature has the power to heal our body, mind and soul. There is plenty of evidence to prove this in numerous studies that have been undertaken over the years. Regular doses of time spent in nature is proven to reduce anxiety, stress and depression. Many techniques are used to help people heal by connecting with Mother Nature and living in balance and harmony with the seasons and cycles of life.

One of the best ways to ground and connect with the Earth is to walk barefoot, whether that is on the grass or dirt. Connecting to the surface of the Earth in this way neutralises your electrical energies. It improves your overall wellbeing and aids healing and repair of bodily systems, preventing disease.

Barefoot walking is very calming for your mind and rejuvenates your senses. You also receive a free reflexology session from Mother Earth, stimulating your entire body through the acupressure points on your feet that correspond to different organs within your body, restoring balance within.

Also, soaking in the sunshine uplifts our spirits and gives us direct natural prana that can sustain us throughout the whole day. We absorb vitamin D from the sun which is necessary for our body and minds to be healthy.

Getting into the habit of spending time outdoors is a very healthy practice to adopt, especially when the weather is improving and the nights are lighter for longer. Get into the routine of taking a break from the hustle and bustle and give yourself time to enjoy the beauty and healing power of being in nature. Take a walk through the woods or near some water. Inhale the delicious scents of the plants and flowers as they bring colour and vibrancy to the environment. Do some gardening. Even five minutes sat in the garden is healing for the soul. Connect with all the elements and the deva kingdom, tuning in to the fairies and nature spirits. Feel the peacefulness and Oneness of everything within and around you. The best thing about nature is that it is free and easily accessible.

What are you waiting for?
There's no time like the present.

Go and enjoy some nature time!

Nutritional Therapy

The food we eat contains information for us to digest and assimilate. The energy vibrations of food interact with all layers of our being. As we ingest food particles, we have the potential to restore balance and harmony to all of our cells.

There are two ways we can look at nourishing the chakras with the foods we eat. Firstly, the colour of the food directly relates to the colour of the chakra bringing balance to that particular energy centre. The colour of food balances each of our chakras through the resonance of vibration. Secondly, different food types also bring balance to each chakra depending on their qualities.

All foods have a unique signature that can have a positive or negative impact on our health. No two people are the same, one man's health is another man's poison. This cleanse will help you to understand your unique mind-body type so you can adjust your diet and find what foods are optimum for you.

Sound Therapy

Sound therapy is used to heal and rejuvenate us on every level. A 'mantra', which means to liberate one's mind, creates transformation on every level of our existence. The rhythm and sound of mantras work on a subconscious level and are very powerful.

When we use intentions with our mantras, the meaning infuses into our consciousness on a deeper level. Chant your mantra and repeat your intentions every morning and the qualities will reverberate silently in the mind and body all day long.

The bija mantras are one syllable sounds that activate and balance the chakras. By repeating the mantras of each chakra, you resonate with that energy to purify and balance the body and mind.

The biji mantras contain the essence and secrets of the chakras

Each biji mantra has both the letters A and M. The M in each of the sounds represents the material and maternal aspects of the Universe. The A sound represents the non-material and paternal aspects.

<u>Colour & Chakra Balancing</u>

Each colour has its own unique meaning and energy. We can change our vibrations including what we think and feel by using colours to help heal us on every level. Crystals help to harmonise our internal energies and can aid in the balancing of each of our chakras.

<u>Aromatherapy</u>

Aromatherapy is a complementary therapy that uses natural plant extracts to promote health and wellbeing. Aromatherapy assists the body's natural ability to heal.

Essential oils have different properties that can support optimum health and wellbeing in body, mind, heart and soul. Independently tested therapeutic-grade essential oils are rigorously tested and are the highest quality and purest essential oils to assist in healing the physical, mental, emotional and spiritual bodies. They do this by raising the vibrations to restore balance on a deep cellular level. These essential oils are nature's medicine.

Archangels

Angels are celestial beings unbound by the physical laws of Earth. They are androgynous and can appear to us in male or female form.

Archangels are the messengers of God who oversee guardian angels and assist lightworkers with their mission on Earth. Some Archangels may be distinctively male or female, such as Michael, who is indomitably male, and Haniel, who is gracefully depicted as female. Others may switch more freely between gender association. Archangels are associated with the chakras and can assist us to restore balance to each of the energy centres. There are many interpretations of Angels and the corresponding chakras, there's no right or wrong way. If a different angel appears to you at a different chakra go with it, this is your personal experience.

Muladhara – Root Chakra – Nourish – Physical Health

Muladhara, our first chakra, resonates with the colour red and the element of Earth. Situated at the base of the spine, muladhara is the energy centre that represents our physical health. This chakra connects us to the material plane of existence and our ability to manifest our needs. The inner state of this chakra is stillness, stability, security and safety. When balanced, you will have a healthy body, feel grounded, strong, courageous, stable, secure and have an abundance of energy and vitality.

The Symbol Meaning of Muladhara

The vermillion lotus blossom at muladhara has four petals around a square. The square is yellow and represents the Earth. Each of the red petals represents the four directions and fundamental psychic functions; the mind, intellect, ego and consciousness. The inverted triangle at muladhara indicates that we are at the beginning of our spiritual journey, the sides of the triangle opening upwards signifies the awakening of our consciousness.

Muladhara is the seat of our dormant wisdom, where our kundalini power resides. Our spiritual abilities and gifts are hidden within muladhara. The kundalini wraps around the Shiva Lingam (the dormant universal consciousness) 3 and a half times, representing the 3 gunas and transcendence. Once we awaken this energy, we begin our journey to spiritual ascension. The animal associated with muladhara is a 7 trunked elephant, representing the sacred 7's. The 7 main chakras, colours of the rainbow, days of the week, notes and the spiritual laws. The number 7 guides us to the vibration of our best Self.

Anatomy & Physiology of Muladhara

Muladhara governs the skeletal and digestive systems. The nerve plexus of muladhara is the sacral plexus, a network of nerve fibres that supplies the muscles and skin of the pelvis and lower limbs. The nerve roots L4 - S4 form the sacral plexus and there are several nerves that stem from the sacral plexus including the sciatic nerve. Grounding poses help to balance the root chakra and helps to free up any blockages within the sacral plexus.

The endocrine gland of muladhara are the adrenal glands, situated on top of each kidney. They work hand in hand with the pituitary gland and hypothalamus. They secrete hormones that regulate metabolism and are responsible for the 'fight, flight or freeze' response. The adrenal glands support our parasympathetic nervous system which helps us to feel grounded and full of vitality when balanced. Working on this chakra will help to strengthen your foundations, balance your adrenal glands and release fear.

Physical imbalance in this chakra relates to lower back, hip and leg pain, constipation, diarrhoea, piles, colitis, cold fingers and toes.

Psychology of Muladhara

Muladhara is the energy centre of physical health. It represents the unconscious mind. Emotional and mental signs that indicate this chakra is out of balance include; feeling insecure, self-pitying, ignorance, restless, selfish, aggressive and lacking in energy. These are all lower aspects of the root chakra that require balancing so you can move into the higher aspects of muladhara, raise your consciousness and free yourself from suffering.

Tamasic personalities of muladhara live in constant fear and perceive the world to be a dangerous place, they are in the lowest vibration of this chakra. People who worry a lot are tamasic with some rajasic qualities. This type of person suffers with anxiety and drops down into a tamasic state when they experience stress. The influence of rajas motivates them to seek relief and continue with their lives. When the influence of rajas increases beyond tamas, a person is ruled by selfish behaviours, they seek to accumulate money and possessions to fill the void they feel inside. Rajasic-dominant people see opportunities in the world and feel secure financially. They are still governed by selfish behaviour, but they include their family and friends in their wealth.

As sattva illuminates within our consciousness, we start to see the bigger picture and become more generous. With rajas still dominating the sattva qualities, this type of personality still has a "what is in it for me?" mentality. Their generosity is conditional. Once sattva becomes stronger than rajas, they realise that acquiring money and possessions doesn't provide security and happiness, feeling secure and happy are internal qualities that are experienced once our basic needs are satisfied.

People who embody sattvic qualities in muladhara are a channel of Divine grace, they do not doubt their security, they feel safe and trust in the higher power. This type of person flows through life noticing beauty and synchronicity everywhere they look.

Once you experience the unity of Oneness and understand that everything is in Divine perfect order, you experience the indescribable enlightened state of muladhara.

Balancing Muladhara – Nourish – Physical Health

Your physical health relates directly to your body and the connection you have with the physical world. In order for us to maintain a healthy body, it is important to re-establish our connection to Mother Earth, nourishing our body with the beauty she provides for us. You can do this by eating a wholesome diet and also spending time in nature to raise your vibration, clear your mind and get rid of negative energy. Practice yoga directly on the earth with bare feet on the grass, feel your roots grow deep into the ground as you connect with the trees and beautiful nature surrounding you. This is great for strengthening the root chakra and your foundations. Another great way to connect with your root chakra is by massaging your feet and showing them some love; after all, they carry you through life and get you to where you need to be.

Nutritional Therapy

Red foods are fantastic for stimulating and energising the root chakra and balancing the physical body. Watermelon is good for the immune system, eyes, skin and hair. This hydrating fruit contains around 92% water and contains vitamins A, C, B1, B5, B6, magnesium and potassium.

Proteins give us strength and are associated with the structural tissue of our root chakra. Proteins provide a solid foundation to keep the first chakra grounded and strong. A vegetarian diet with adequate amounts of protein will keep this chakra balanced. Foods to include are lentils, pulses, beans, legumes, tofu, nuts, non-dairy milks and cheeses (dairy products if you are not vegan).

Root vegetables are also great for this chakra as they help to ground you to the Earth. Potatoes, carrots, parsnips, turnips, beets, yams, celery, horseradish, artichokes, onions, garlic, turmeric and ginger are all healthy roots to include in your diet. These vegetables also balance your heart chakra and strengthen your system as a whole.

Mantra: LAM – The sound of Spiritual Awakening

LAM cleanses the root chakra of impurities, opening you up to feeling safe and secure. It removes blockages, releases tension, eliminates fear and activates kundalini energy. Deep hurts and disappointments are buried at muladhara. When we awaken the energy here, our deeply buried trauma and pain come to the surface so they can be healed and resolved. We transform our negative experiences into valuable life lessons and opportunities for development. Learning from our experiences helps us to grow and evolve, breaking away from the cycle of pain and suffering.

Colour & Crystal Therapy

Red is a hot colour that is often associated with danger. It has the longest wavelength closest to infrared on the electromagnetic spectrum. Red increases energy, vitality and confidence and has a grounding effect on our physical body. Surrounding yourself with the colour red, wearing red and eating red foods increase the body's ability to absorb iron, having a positive effect on the blood and circulatory system.

The properties of red, brown or black crystals ground and balance this chakra. Garnet is the finest energising stone for the body as it amplifies the properties of other crystals. Not only does this stone harmonize muladhara, it can also be used on other chakras that are underactive to increase their energy.

Red garnet stimulates kundalini rising and is a great stone to use especially at the beginning of your spiritual journey. This stone brings courage and strengthens the survival instinct which is needed to balance the root chakra and our foundations.

Ruby is an energising stone that is known as the stone of the sun in ayurvedic healing. It is great for detoxifying the body and mind of impurities and negative energies. It has a very powerful effect on the blood and circulatory system. Ruby promotes dynamic energy, abundance and wealth, making it a great stone to balance muladhara. It also balances and stimulates the heart chakra.

Other crystals that bring balance to the root chakra include; rhodochrosite, red jasper, red calcite, coral, smoky quartz, onyx and black tourmaline.

Aromatherapy

Essential oils from trees are very grounding and great for strengthening the root chakra.

Vetiver is the oil of descent and centering. Connecting us to the physical world, vetiver grounds us in the present moment and helps us to discover the deeper facets of who we are. It connects us deeply to our thoughts and feelings, and supports a healthy nervous system. Other essential oils that are good for muladhara include; cedarwood, douglas fir and black spruce.

Archangel Michael: Warrior of Strength

Archangel Michael (he who is God), is the leader of all the Archangels. He is a powerful Archangel who protects us from fear and phobias. Michael strengthens our courage and faith and helps us to break away from negative people and situations. You can call upon Archangel Michael to cut away any cords between you and other people to break bonds that are causing you hurt and pain. Archangel Michael helps us to cleanse and strengthen our root chakra removing any fear from our energy field.

Swadhistana - Sacral Chakra – Create – Emotional Wellbeing

Swadhistana, our second chakra, resonates with the colour orange and the element of water. Situated just below and behind the navel, swadhistana is the energy centre that represents our emotional wellbeing. The energy of swadhsitana is free-flowing, fluid and always moving. Our initial unity from muladhara now becomes duality and we find a desire to connect with others, our emotions, sensuality and sexuality. When balanced, we feel happy, enthusiastic, independent, sociable, creative and emotionally balanced able to express ourselves clearly.

<u>Symbol Meaning of Swadhistana</u>

The sacral lotus flower is symbolic for the cycle of birth, death and re-birth. The vermillion lotus blossom at swadhistana has 6 petals. On each petal there is a letter; bam, bham, mam, yam, ram and lam.

The crescent moon symbol represents the water element of this chakra and the animals associated here are water animals. The fish represents Parvati and crocodile represents Vishnu.

Anatomy & Physiology of Swadhistana

Swadhistana governs our reproductive organs. The nerve plexus of swadhistana is the hypogastric plexus, which consists of 2 parts; the superior and inferior plexuses. Grounding poses help to balance the hypogastric plexus.

The endocrine glands of swadhistana are the ovaries and testes. These reproductive glands secrete sex hormones and control sexual development. Reclining butterfly pose is great for regulating the sex hormones and balancing swadhistana.

Physical signs this chakra is out of balance include: problems with ovaries or testes, PMS, IBS, endometriosis, sex issues and depression. Pain in the lumbar area and pelvis also indicates imbalance of swadhistana. When energy becomes blocked at the sacral chakra, we feel stagnant, lethargic and lacking in energy.

Psychology of Swadhistana

Swadhistana is the energy centre of emotional wellbeing. It represents the subconscious mind. Emotional and mental signs that indicate this chakra is out of balance include; feeling unhappy, disconnected from emotions, withdrawn, egotistic, doubtful, anxious, guilty, destructive, and can be over-dependent.

Tamasic personalities of swadhistana are negative and pessimistic. This type of person has very low energy and self-esteem, they experience extreme sadness and are unable to enjoy life. Addictions can be a problem for people in a tamasic-rajasic state. When the influence of rajas becomes more dominant than tamas, they are motivated to break away from addictive behaviours, but the tamas can still have a hold and pull them back down into the lower aspects of this chakra.

Rajasic personalities are happy, positive and like to have fun. They seek pleasure from external influences and have not yet realised that happiness is an inside job. When sattva becomes stronger than rajas, they begin to realise that happiness and joy comes from within.

Sattvic people radiate joy. They see the good in everything and everyone and are able to bring out the best in people. Once we embody Oneness with the Divine, we enter into the enlightened qualities of swadhistana and experience pure ecstatic bliss.

Balancing Swadhistana – Create – Emotional Wellbeing

Connect with the element of water to restore balance to this chakra. Swadhistana represents movement; its purpose is to let go and flow. Increasing your energy levels and being more active will free up trapped energy in this chakra, especially creating movement in the pelvis. Healing this chakra requires you to be in touch with your emotions and express them in healthy ways. By observing emotions, you can process and learn from them. Accept how you feel, and use the experience as a chance to grow and evolve.

Working on the lower aspects of swadhistana will shift you from the victim mentality of feeling hopeless and powerless, opening your consciousness so you can move into the higher aspects of this chakra. Being creative and focusing on seeing the bigger picture will help to restore this chakra to its optimum functioning.

Nutritional Therapy

Orange foods restore the sacral chakra. Carrots help to heal and cure the body. Carrot juice is a powerful blood cleaner and muscle builder, it boosts the immune system and protects against disease. Carrots contain vitamins A, B, C, D, E and K and contain many minerals including calcium, copper, iodine, iron, magnesium, manganese, phosphorus, potassium, sodium and sulphur. Oranges are a good source of fibre, vitamin C, B vitamins and antioxidants.

Swadhisthana is associated with all liquids in the diet including water, herbal teas, juices and oils. It is important to have lots of fluids throughout the day to keep this chakra balanced and to flush out toxins from the body. Make sure you drink plenty of water throughout the day. Aim for 2 litres of water including herbal teas. Ginger and turmeric tea is a fantastic drink for cleansing the body and balancing the sacral chakra.

Oils transport essential nutrients around the body keeping our systems strong and healthy. Coconut oil, avocado oil, milk thistle oil, hemp oil and extra virgin olive oil are examples of healthy oils to include in your diet.

Mantra: VAM – Awakens the flowing energy of swadhistana, awakening our emotions that rise from subconscious into our consciousness. Suppressing emotions causes imbalance in the system and can create disharmony in the mind and body. To free ourselves from these feelings we must shine a light on them, and remove them with wisdom and compassion. Chanting this mantra helps us to transform negative emotions into something more positive and beautiful.

Colour & Crystal Therapy

Orange is a dynamic colour that holds a mixture of red and yellow blending the properties of both primary colours.

Orange is associated with fire and is warm without the burning hot sensation of red. It has a creative energy bringing playfulness and enjoyment. For this reason, it is great for removing blockages and keeping the energy flowing. The colour orange represents instinctive energy and enables us to put our thoughts into practice in the world creatively. Surrounding yourself with the colour orange, wearing orange clothes and crystals, and eating orange foods balances the sacral chakra and your emotions.

Orange crystals are warming, they bring balance and harmony to the sacral chakra. The rays of orange crystals unblock the energy flow of this chakra bringing balance to your emotional Self so you can trust in the flow of life. Carnelian stimulates creativity and is one of the best stones for healing the etheric body. It is full of life force and increases the vitality of the whole body, especially the reproductive organs. It also aids in overcoming negative conditioning, clearing the mind so you can trust in yourself and your own instincts.

Orange citrine balances the sacral chakra and encourages the flow of creativity along with clear thoughts and improved memory. Orange topaz is great for calming the emotions and releasing tension. Other orange crystals that balance swadhistana include; beryll, orange kyanite and tangerine aura quartz.

Do something creative like paint, draw or write to stimulate your creative energy to balance this chakra whilst having your crystal close by. Tune into your chosen crystal and feel the energy emanating throughout your aura and absorbing into your body changing your energy field. Meditate with it and empower your creative emotional Self on a deeper level.

Aromatherapy

Wild orange is the oil of abundance. It opens the creative channels and reconnects us with our childlike sense of wonder and awe. Wild orange encourages fun, playfulness and spontaneity. We are truly abundant in all ways. This oil reminds us of our Divine nature and our natural state of limitless abundance. Other essential oils that are good for swadhistana include; geranium, spearmint and roman chamomile.

Archangel Haniel: Warrior of Love

Archangel Haniel is the Angel of Divine grace and joy. She is associated with the moon and Venus, the planet of love. Haniel offers support to women during their monthly cycles. Her gentle soothing energy assists in healing emotional pain, and connecting us to higher wisdom.

Manipura – Solar Plexus – Empower – Mental Awareness

Manipura, our third chakra, resonates with the colour yellow and the element of fire. Situated just below and behind the breastbone, this energy centre represents our mental health. Manipura is the seat of our personal power, which allows us to destroy illusions and realise higher levels of truth. This fiery solar energy brings us light, warmth, energy, power and vitality. When balanced, we feel optimistic, energetic, alert, authoritative, confident and in control of our lives, unaffected by negativity and criticism.

Symbol Meaning of Manipura

Manipura is a 10 petalled lotus blossom. Each petal represents one of the ten pranas, our life force energy. These pranas are divided into 2 groups of 5, prana vayus and upa pranas.

They regulate the functioning of all our organs and bodily systems. The basic functions of the body, prana (life force) and apana (elimination of waste) meet at manipura; they represent the assimilation and elimination, the giving and receiving. These pranas are not only affected by the oxygen that we breathe and the foods we eat, our thoughts, feelings and individual qualities also affect this pranic energy. The animal associated with manipura is the ram, which represents physical strength, stamina and endurance.

Anatomy & Physiology of Manipura

Manipura governs the muscular, metabolic and digestive systems. The nerve plexus of manipura is the solar plexus, a network of nerves situated below the diaphragm behind the stomach. It is the largest autonomic nerve centre in the abdomen cavity, with lots of interconnected neurons and ganglia. Breath awareness at the solar plexus will help to relax and balance this nerve plexus.

The endocrine gland of manipura is the pancreas, which is situated below and behind the stomach and has two parts. The endocrine pancreas secretes hormones that regulate blood glucose levels, and the exocrine pancreas secretes digestive enzymes. It also regulates metabolism.

Physical signs of imbalance include; diabetes, liver disease, pancreatitis, gall stones and inflammation of the digestive tract.

Psychology of Manipura

Manipura is the energy centre of mental awareness, it represents the conscious mind. Emotional and mental signs that indicate this chakra is out of balance include; feeling indecisive, pessimistic, sarcastic, angry, over analytical and unfocused.

Tamasic personalities of manipura are lazy, lethargic and dull. They are procrastinators and lack the ability to get going. With the influence of rajas, these people have the motivation get going, but the tamas drags them down and holds them back from completing anything. This type of person rarely finishes projects and usually feels guilty as a result. When the influence of rajas becomes stronger than tamas, motivation is higher, but this personality type tends to lose interest and can give up before completing their projects which can create anger and destructiveness in their lives.

Rajasic personalities tend to have a healthy manipura chakra with good energy flow and vitality. They are competitive, ambitious and opportunists. These people are quick to help others, but they always seek personal gain from experiences and want to know 'what is in it for them'. Once sattva starts flowing into manipura, they work purposefully for the greater good without expecting anything in return. They are aligned with their dharma and following their passion and calling.

When the influence of sattva increases beyond rajas, the love from anahata flows freely onto manipura and this person offers their services to the world to help others.

Sattvic people realise they are a channel of Divine grace. Life flows effortlessly and in accordance with Divine will. Not only was manipura my most dominant chakra throughout life, until my awakening, it was the first of my chakras to naturally move into a sattvic nature. One fine day, the light of sattva flooded my consciousness whilst I was deep in meditation at The Monastery of St. Francis in Gorton. I sat peacefully, an open channel for the

Divine and the words of St. Francis flowed into my heart and changed my life forever.

"Lord, make me an instrument of thy peace" St. Francis

On realisation of the true powers of the universe and the interconnection between everything and everyone, we move into an enlightened state of consciousness.

Balancing Manipura – Empower – Mental Awareness

Working on the solar plexus chakra balances the mental body and personal power. The powers are amplified and have the greatest benefit when practiced in bright sunlight with the healing energy of the sun.

Manipura is the transformation centre where we can burn away lower energies and transmute them into positive energy. Once we burn away our insecurities and negative aspects in the fire of manipura, we move into the higher aspects of the chakra and claim the powerful "I AM" presence. The "I AM" presence is identity of the true Self and realisation of your Divine nature. The "I AM" presence goes by many names including; Brahma, God, Allah, Great Spirit and Holy Creator. By claiming your power, you can transform your negative habits into more empowering thoughts, feelings and beliefs and manifest your dream life.

Nutritional Therapy

Manipura relates to the element of fire and digestion. This chakra coverts starches into energy. To keep manipura healthy, it is important to consume wholegrains and avoid processed flours. Wholegrain foods are assimilated by the body more slowly and are nourishing for the body on every level. They are high in fibre, easy to digest, satisfying and loaded with nutrients. Wholegrain foods help us to control blood sugar levels and bring balance to this chakra. To keep manipura healthy and vibrant, include wholegrain bread, rice, oats, quinoa, millet, barley and cous cous in your diet. Of all the starches, quinoa is one of the most nutrient dense and the only carbohydrate that is a complete protein. Add mung beans and lentils to your rice to make the dish a complete protein, which will also have a grounding effect strengthening your root chakra.

Pineapple is my favourite juice for balancing the solar plexus chakra. Not only are pineapples packed with vitamins, minerals and antioxidants, they also contain Bromelain, an enzyme found in the core of the pineapple which is used as medicine. This enzyme causes the body to produce substances which fight inflammation and pain.

Pineapples contain manganese, which is a trace mineral that your body needs to build strong healthy bones and connective tissues. I like to add mango and passionfruit, which also assists the sacral chakra and makes it taste even more tropical and tasty!

Mantra: RAM – Awakens manipura and radiates warmth through the body. It is here where we burn away negative energy and transmute it into something positive and good.

"Om mani padme hum" is a great mantra to use for manipura. It means "I am the jewel in the lotus, carrying all the jewels as Divine qualities within". This mantra frees us from inner problems and our demons, guiding us to self-realisation and enlightenment.

Colour & Crystal Therapy

Yellow is a bright vibrant colour that we can associate with the sun. The morning sun is stimulating and energising for plants, animals and all living beings. Different shades of yellow have their own unique properties. Lighter shades of yellow clear the mind, and at the same time keep it alert and active. The brighter shades hold a stronger vibration than the lighter shades, they stimulate and energise the body and mind. Yellow encourages decision making, orderliness and clarity. The digestive, immune and nervous systems all have yellow frequencies. Without this colour vibration present in daily life, the system as a whole becomes disturbed and illness and disease can manifest.

The rays of yellow crystals restore balance to this chakra. They energise and stimulate manipura and help to support positivity.

Tiger's eye awakens the energy at the solar plexus increasing willpower. It is also used to resolve conflicts and brings peace of mind. This stone is commonly used to treat mental health disorders and is great for lifting moods. As the energy increases with this stone, the lower chakras synchronize and stimulate the kundalini.

Yellow citrine also balances manipura, increasing self-confidence and will-power. It is a great crystal to promote relaxation of the body and mind and for increasing optimism. The bright yellow energy of this stone calms the digestive system and soothes the nervous system.

Amber has a gentler energy that is soothing and balancing for the nervous system. It is a stone for detoxification.

Other yellow stones for balancing manipura include pyrite and fire opal.

Aromatherapy

Cardamom, the oil of objectivity and mental sobriety is great for manipura. It helps to balance the mind and develop self-control. Cardamom reduces frustration and anger, and re-directs emotional energy to the solar plexus, the centre of willpower, responsibility and transformation where lower vibrational energies can be transmuted in the fire.

Other essential oils which are good for manipura include; ginger, lemon, lemongrass, bergamot and black pepper.

Archangel Ariel: Warrior of Transformation

Archangel Ariel, also known as the “Lioness of God”, is the angel of nature. She can help us connect with the natural world and the elemental kingdom. Tune into the elements and call upon Archangel Ariel to help you discern your true purpose in life.

Anahata – Heart Chakra – Love – Unity Consciousness

Anahata, our fourth chakra, resonates with the colour green and the element of air. Situated in the centre of the chest, anahata represents unity consciousness and healthy relationships. This chakra is the central point in our energy system, our spiritual centre that unites forces from above and below. It is here we find Divine love and infinite bliss in the union with our true Self. When balanced, we feel unconditional love for ourselves and others, and live in harmony with Mother Nature and the whole Universe. We have good relationships and act with kindness and compassion.

Symbol Meaning of Anahata

Anahata is a twelve petalled lotus blossom, each petal representing the twelve qualities we are able to develop in the heart centre:

Peace, love, joy, compassion, forgiveness, kindness, understanding, bliss, harmony, clarity, purity and patience.

Once we open and awaken these twelve qualities, we truly start living with an open heart. By devoting our lives to spiritual practice, these twelve petals blossom into the celestial flower of universal love. The opening of anahata enriches our lives with love, peace of mind and inner fulfilment.

The symbols of anahata are a six-pointed star and a new moon which represent the changes we experience when we awaken this centre. The star is formed with two triangles, one tip pointing upwards symbolising the Shakti energy and the raising of our consciousness. The other tip pointing downwards implying we can easily slip back down into the lower chakras as we struggle with our negative qualities and habits.

The new moon represents the beginning of expanded awareness, the start of a new journey into higher states of consciousness. The animal associated with the heart chakra is the antelope, symbolising transformation and freedom. Antelopes fly through the air in great leaps, moving as if they have wings. These beautiful animals closely resemble unicorns, a symbol of magic.

Anatomy & Physiology of Anahata

Anahata governs the respiratory, circulatory and immune systems. The nerve plexus of anahata is the cardiac plexus, which is situated around the base of the heart and is formed by the cardiac branches from the vagus nerves and sympathetic trunk and ganglia. It consists of various sympathetic, parasympathetic and afferent fibres and is divided into superficial and deep parts. Practicing giving and receiving love relaxes and balances the cardiac plexus.

The endocrine gland of anahata is the thymus gland, situated behind the sternum just above the heart. It is the master gland of the immune system that produces white blood cells to fight infections and destroy unhealthy cells. With the heart chakra being the central point of our existence, we can strengthen our thymus gland by practicing loving kindness and compassion to ourselves and others.

Physical signs this chakra is out of balance include; heart disease, breathing difficulties, immune system disorders and allergies.

Psychology of Anahata

Anahata is the centre where we develop unity consciousness. The role of this chakra is to integrate and balance the various aspects of our being, so that we feel whole. The heart chakra is the union of male and female energies and integrates the physical word of matter (lower chakras) with the wonderful world of Spirit (upper chakras). Our ego and lower 3 chakras are physical and individual. Our soul and upper 3 chakras are spiritual and collective. The lower and upper aspects of us meet at the heart chakra, uniting our body, mind, heart and spirit. The essence of the entire cosmos exists in our heart chakra.

Emotional and mental signs that indicate this chakra is out of balance include; feeling bitterness, jealousy, misery, over-dependent, unloving and indifference. Feeling like you do not deserve love and taking on other peoples' emotions and problems as your own are lower aspects of this chakra. Once you awaken your heart to Divine love, your vibrations raise exponentially and you reach the higher aspects of this chakra.

Tamasic personalities of anahata are submerged in apathy and feel isolated from the world. This type of person sees kindness as weakness, they live a lonely existence. With the influence of rajas, they tend to be anti-social and usually fall into the wrong groups of people such as criminals and drug addicts. When the influence of rajas becomes dominant over tamas, they feel motivated to change and improve their lives.

Rajasic personalities seek love outside of themselves. Their love is conditional, they haven't yet realised that their very nature is pure love. This type of person is looking for their other half to complete them instead of becoming whole themselves.

Once sattva starts to shine through, they become more loving and compassionate for others. When sattva becomes stronger than rajas, they see the world differently and seek out ways to help those who are finding life difficult; they want to make a difference in the world.

Sattvic personalities are pure love. Their natural state of love radiates from their hearts and dissolves anything that isn't love in an instant. These people are surrounded by loving people, they make a difference in the world by being their true authentic Self. Once cosmic love is experienced and all that is not love is dissolved, you move into a blissful state of ecstatic love and enlightened consciousness.

Balancing Anahata – Love – Unity Consciousness

The heart chakra yearns to let go, surrendering into peace and harmony. To balance your heart chakra, it is important to let go of all that no longer serves you and open your heart to unconditional love and compassion. The energy you send out into the world comes back to you tenfold. Give out love and allow that same unconditional love to come back to you from the world around and within you. Be kind to all Earth's inhabitants including animals, creatures, trees and plants. Practice giving and receiving to open your heart chakra. Pranayama is an important technique for the heart chakra, especially when dealing with painful memories. If our ego is unable to digest and assimilate negativity, the pain and suffering remains in the heart centre lowering our vibrations and holding us back from achieving higher states of consciousness.

<u>Nutritional Therapy for Anahata: Vegetables</u>

Vegetables contain a high amount of prana, natural life force. All vegetables absorb the vital energy of the sunlight (fire), along with a balance of the other elements, earth, water and air. When we consume vegetables, we are taking in the cosmic energy of the Universe and if we listen closely, our food gives us messages forming the person we become.

Include an abundance of vegetables in your diet to awaken and balance your heart chakra. Include plenty of organic dark green leafy vegetables such as kale, spinach, chard, rocket, lettuce, collards, dandelion, mustard greens, turnip greens, broccoli, courgettes, sprouts, cauliflower, cabbage, bok choy, peas, peppers, leeks and watercress.

Spinach is anti-inflammatory and is great for bone health. It has an amazing array of nutrients, including high amounts of iron, magnesium, calcium, folate, vitamins A, C and K. The high iron content helps to transport oxygen around the body, promoting healing to damaged tissues and removing toxic waste.

I love starting my day with a green smoothie. The liquid nature cleanses the sacral chakra and the protein in the greens grounds the root chakra. You can add spices such as cinnamon or cayenne pepper to boost metabolism and energise your solar plexus chakra. Add a little fruit and you also enter into the dimensions of your first spiritual chakra, the throat chakra. And there you have it, cleansing all the chakras in one delicious smoothie, what a fantastic way to start your day!

Mantra: YAM - The sound of the Universe. The eternal vibration of the true Self resides in anahata.

<u>Colour & Crystal Therapy</u>

Green is found midway in the spectrum and is the peaceful colour of nature. It represents growth and change. We can see this in the transformation of nature changing from one season to the next. Green is the energy of finding new direction and new paths. It brings balance and harmony to our lives and relationships.

We have 2 chakras at the heart centre, the second being the higher heart that vibrates a pink frequency. If you have been working with chakras for some time, you may naturally see and feel pink light instead of green whilst working through anahata chakra. This is fantastic, follow your instincts and let love guide you.

The energy of green and pink crystals balances and harmonises the heart chakra and offers calming influences. Amazonite opens the heart and heals the body and mind. It is a great stone for releasing blockages and negative energy from the whole system. It also absorbs electromagnetic pollution from our environment. This crystal brings balance to all of our energies, masculine/feminine, yin/yang, physical/spiritual.

Jade brings peace and tranquillity to the heart chakra increasing love and compassion. It is great for soothing the mind and releasing negative thoughts and emotions. This stone awakens you to your spiritual Self and encourages you to integrate all aspects of your being.

Chalcedony is a beautiful stone that brings harmony to the body, mind and spirit. It is good to use in a group to promote connection. Other crystals that balance anahata include; emerald, malachite, tourmaline, peridot, moss agate, bloodstone and rose quartz.

Aromatherapy

Geranium is the oil of love and connection. It brings you deeply into the heart and away from the logical mind. Geranium helps to heal emotional wounds and aids in healing a broken heart. Other essential oils that are good for anahata include; rose, peppermint, eucalyptus, lemongrass and basil.

Archangel Raphael: Warrior of Healing

Archangel Raphael is the supreme powerful angel of healing. You can call upon Raphael to heal physical, mental and emotional illness. He will support you on your healing journey and improve your health and wellbeing. He is the chief of the guardian angels.

Vishuddhi – Throat Chakra – Share – Authentic Expression

Vishuddhi, our fifth chakra, resonates with the colour blue and the element of space and sound. Situated in the throat, vishuddhi is the first of the spiritual chakras. It is the energy center of authentic expression and relates to communication between our inner and outer worlds. When balanced, we feel calm, expressive, creative, inspired, loyal, trustworthy and graceful, have great communication skills and are able to express ourselves clearly. We hear the voice of our higher Self and angels more easily.

Symbol Meaning of Vishuddhi

The lotus blossom of vishuddhi has 16 petals. Each one represents the 16 supernatural powers (siddhis) that can be acquired through the practice of yoga. These siddhis are to be used only in harmony with Divine will, or else yogic powers will be lost.

The animal associated with the throat chakra is a white elephant, representing strength, prosperity, wisdom, purity and good luck.

Anatomy & Physiology of Vishuddhi

The throat chakra governs the endocrine and respiratory systems. The nerve plexus of vishuddhi is the carotid plexus, a network of intersecting sympathetic nerves that run parallel to the carotid artery into the head. Ujjayi (throat breathing) helps to balance and restore the carotid plexus.

The endocrine gland of vishuddhi is the thyroid gland. The thyroid gland, situated in the neck, produces a thyroid-stimulating hormone (TSH) which helps to maintain normal blood pressure, heart rate, body temperature and metabolism. Deep breathing techniques help to revitalise the thyroid and parathyroid glands.

Physical signs this chakra is out of balance include; sore throat, tonsillitis, thyroid problems, lung problems and asthma.

Psychology of Vishuddhi

Vishuddhi is the energy centre of authentic expression and higher consciousness. It is the border between physical and astral levels, between consciousness and super-consciousness. The throat chakra is where we open up to our spiritual gifts and develop trust and deeper connections to the Spirit realm.

When we enter into the throat chakra, we tune into the subtle vibrations of the world around us and start to perceive things from an energetic point of view. By tuning into the resonant rhythm of life, we integrate the core of our being with the heart of the Universe. The energy and vibrations within us affect everything around us and we pick up on other peoples' thoughts, feelings and emotions. As this is on a subtle level and we cannot see it with our physical eyes, we are rarely conscious of these energetic interactions and our vibrations and mood can change without us understanding why. Awareness at vishuddhi helps us to discern our feelings from others so we can stay in higher vibrations and protect our energy from absorbing negativity from our surroundings. For us to truly connect with the world, we must be able to entrain with the vibrational frequencies around us. Emotional and mental signs that indicate this chakra is out of balance include; feeling cold, untrustworthy, unfaithful, self-righteous and have trouble expressing Oneself.

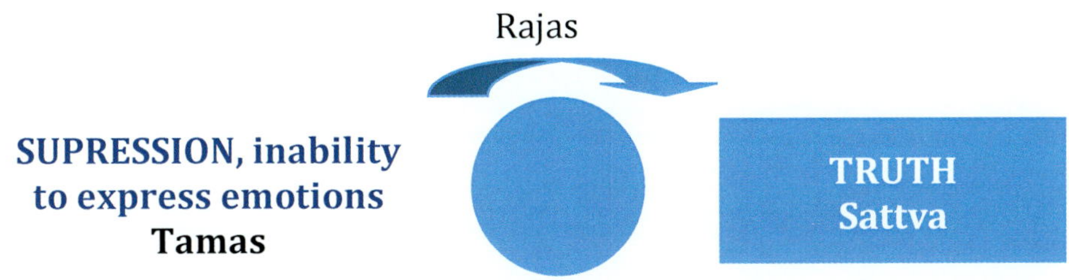

Tamasic personalities of vishuddhi are isolated and alienated from people. They are not very good at communicating and are typical loners. With the influence of rajas, this person is not so much a loner, but they lack communication skills and let everyone else do the talking. When the influence of rajas increases beyond tamas, the communication flows freely. These people generally speak too much and can be very negative, often complaining about anything and everything.

Rajasic personalities tend to communicate really well. They can be good listeners when the chakra is balanced. If vishuddhi is really active they can be very chatty and dominate conversations. Once sattva starts to shine through, a person becomes articulate and communicates with clarity. This type of person is highly intuitive.

Once we open up to the cosmic energy and become a channel of Divine grace, information flows through us from the higher levels. The sattvic personality type is intuitive and wise with great ability to communicate with large groups.

An enlightened vishuddhi realises the power of thoughts and words. At this level, we are very aware of our thoughts, words and actions, as we know the power they possess. A single word can change the trajectory of your life!

Balancing Vishuddhi – Share – Authentic Expression

To balance vishuddhi, connect your physical presence with your spiritual awareness, opening up your consciousness to higher realms of knowledge and wisdom. Throughout the day express your authentic Self through movement and sounds. Sing, sigh, and make animal noises! Anything your heart desires; allow that energy to flow through you uninterrupted.

Nutritional Therapy

Fruits contain a high amount of prana and are very light in nature. When fruit is ripe, it naturally drops to the ground and does not require picking. For this reason, they are considered the purest of all foods. The energy of fruit passes through the system the quickest, and is free to travel to the upper chakras to awaken the higher Self. Include a variety of apples, pears, oranges, grapes, grapefruit, mango, pineapple, kiwi, peaches, banana, papaya, berries, plums, pomegranate, coconut, watermelon, figs, avocado, lemon and limes in your diet.

Blueberries have the highest antioxidant capacity and are great for boosting the immune system and warding off disease. The fibre content in berries are great for the digestive system and for combatting constipation. Blueberries contain manganese, copper, potassium, iron, vitamins C, K, E and B vitamins.

Mantra: HAM - is a light ethereal sound that awakens and balances the throat chakra. Meaning "That I am", we begin to understand who we really are when we work on this chakra.

When our problems arise in vishuddhi, we can either push them back down into our lower chakras and subconscious Self, or purify them and get rid of them for good.

The vibrations of each bija mantra we have been working with becomes lighter and faster as we move up through the chakra system. Today we move up into the first spiritual chakra with sound healing for vishuddhi. You can purify all your negativity here at vishuddhi and realise your beautiful authentic Divine Self and inner powers.

Colour & Crystal Therapy

Blue is a peaceful colour that helps to calm the mind and relax the senses. The energy of blue enhances the flow of communication to express ourselves freely and to also listen and understand our own thoughts and feelings.

Blue is associated with the sky and sea. Both of these elements free the mind and raise the vibrations of the body reducing negativity.

The energy of blue has a cool vibration and can help to reduce the hot vibration of the colour red. Blue also has a sense of detachment and devotion, helping us to let go of all that no longer serves us so we can focus on become our greatest Self.

The energy of blue crystals activates and restores balance to the throat chakra, strengthening the body's defences against illness and disease. Sound is also an important healing modality when working on the throat chakra; any healing on this chakra should be accompanied with soothing music.

Turquoise is a powerful healing stone that regenerates cellular tissues healing the whole body. It is great for strengthening the thymus gland which is one of the main organs of the immune system.

Turquoise strengthens the subtle energy fields, wards off negative energy and offers protection. It is said that the stone changes colour to warn of danger coming.

Aquamarine is a beautiful crystal which is magnificent for strengthening the immune system and recovering from illness. This stone also encourages self-expression and positivity. It is great for balancing throat chakra issues such as a sore throat, swollen glands, tonsillitis and thyroid problems.

Blue lace agate has a soft gentle energy that soothes and cleanses the throat chakra. It is a fantastic stone for healing the body and mind, especially the throat area. The vibrations of this stone bring peace and clarity, calming the mind.

Other crystals that balance vishuddhi include; azurite, lapis lazuli, blue kyanite, sodalite, celestial aura quartz, blue halite and sapphire.

Aromatherapy

Spearmint is the oil of communication and expression. It enables us to translate our inner clarity into words and express it confidently when speaking. This is a great oil to use before giving a speech to ensure you convey your message with clarity and confidence.

Other essential oils that are good for vishuddhi include; lavender and black pepper.

Archangel Gabriel: Warrior of Truth

Archangel Gabriel offers spiritual guidance and assists awakening. His name means, 'Strength of God'. Gabriel is the messenger angel and is the patron of communication. Gabriel inspires creative expression and helps artists, writers and poets with their work.

Ajna – Third Eye Chakra – Imagine – Spiritual Thought

Ajna, our sixth chakra, resonates with the colour indigo and the element of light. Situated between the eyebrows in the centre of the brain, this chakra governs our spiritual thought. Ajna connects us to our intuitive wisdom and inner knowledge. It is in this chakra that we perceive the world and externalise our inner world. Ajna chakra is the home of our spirit within, where darkness and ignorance become One with light and knowledge. When balanced, you will have high concentration, focus and willpower, and feel highly intuitive, idealistic, wise, clear sighted and full of integrity.

Symbol Meaning of Ajna

There are only two petals on the lotus at ajna chakra. They stand for GU (darkness/ignorance) and RU (light/knowledge). The GURU master is formed at the joining and balancing of these two symbols.

These two petals hold the mantras HAM (ida) and KSHAM (pingala) – Shiva and Shakti. Once Shiva and Shakti re-unite at Ajna chakra, the veil of duality is lifted and we feel complete, whole and liberated. The Shiva lingam symbol is present at ajna chakra. In muladhara it is black, whereas here it is a smoky white colour indicating that a lot of purification has been processed but that there is still work to be done. To fully purify this chakra, one must be guided by Bhakti (devotion) to become an enlightened being. The animal associated with the third eye is the owl, the keeper of sacred knowledge, wisdom and intuition.

Anatomy & Physiology of Ajna

The third eye chakra governs the nervous system. The nerve plexus of ajna is the myenteric plexus, a collection of neurons from the ventral part of the brain stem. It originates in the medulla oblongata situated at the upper end of the spinal cord.

The myenteric plexus functions as part of the enteric nervous system which governs the function of the gastrointestinal system (our second brain). Child pose in yoga helps to balance this plexus and calms the entire nervous system.

The endocrine glands of ajna are the pituitary gland and hypothalamus. The pituitary gland and hypothalamus govern the previous five glands and produce hormones that affect all of the other endocrine glands. Nadi shodana (alternate nostril breathing) is a fantastic pranayama technique to balance the pituitary gland and hypothalamus.

Physical signs this chakra is out of balance include; tension headaches, visual defects and problems with eyes, sinuses and ears.

Psychology of Ajna

Ajna chakra is the energy centre of spiritual thought and super consciousness. In the lower states, a person may have difficulty thinking and have no clarity or focus. In the higher states, it is possible unlock your potential, developing intuition and wisdom. Once ajna is open and fully active, profound meaning to life is realised and we access our multi-dimensionality.

Emotional and mental signs that indicate this chakra is out of balance include; being inconsiderate, the inability to trust our intuition and being scattered-minded.

Tamasic personalities have difficulty thinking. With the influence of rajas, this person is able to think logically, but their thoughts can be quite tangled and not very clear. When the influence of rajas becomes stronger than tamas, the energy flows more freely. This person can think more clearly, but they are still clouded by the darker energies of tamas. They are indecisive and quickly jump to conclusions without seeing the bigger picture.

Rajasic personalities are intellectual and logical. They are ambitious and driven by personal desires. They make up the majority of people in society. With the influence of sattva, they see the bigger picture and have great life experiences and memories. This type of person is attracted to knowledge and education and governed by their intellect. Once the influence of sattva becomes stronger than rajas, they tap into their intuition and are able to receive visions and gifts from the higher realms. These creative individuals are unique geniuses.

Sattva personalities are completely aligned with Source and in-tune with their higher Self. They channel wisdom from the Divine and are exceedingly intuitive. At this level of evolvement, psychic powers such as clairvoyance, clairaudience, telepathy and healing can develop. This individual only ever uses their gifts to benefit the planet and the evolution of consciousness for humanity.

An enlightened ajna chakra is one who has realised the profound meaning to life and the secrets of the universe. They realise the multi-dimensional nature of reality and experience the life-changing transformation of their self-realisation.

Balancing Ajna – Imagine – Spiritual Thought

Ida (the feminine lunar) and pingala (the masculine solar) energy channels separate from the sushumna channel at muladhara, intertwine up through all the chakras and reunite at ajna chakra, bringing a sense of Oneness and unity with the entire cosmic Universe. The joining of ida and pingala merging with sushumna signifies the end of duality. This union leads to balance, liberation and contentment.

Through creative visualisation, we can form images in our third eye chakra to manifest things into our reality. Ajna chakra is the seat of our extra-sensory perceptions and gifts of clairvoyance, intuition and telepathy.

To balance ajna chakra, practice connecting to your Spirit within. We all have psychic abilities when we awaken to our Divine nature and tune into the vibrations of the Universe. Lower aspects of ajna chakra include thinking too much and over-analysing things. Calming the mind through meditation will help you to move into the higher aspects of ajna chakra.

Still your mind, and listen intently for Divine guidance. Notice any thoughts and feelings that may arise during the day; this is the angels' way of communicating with you. Release the need to separate things into duality such as; good/bad, right/wrong, black/white etc... Everything is Oneness, we are all connected. Once we move into the higher aspects of ajna, we have the ability to bring new paradigms to Earth, increasing the consciousness of humanity.

Nutritional Therapy

The third eye chakra has a high vibration with very subtle energy that relates to different mental states. The best way to nourish ajna chakra is through pranayama, meditation, prayer and fasting. Blueberries and other dark blue and purple colour foods are also good for balancing ajna chakra. You will love having a nourishing golden milk elixir made from almond milk and spices for your evening meal on the day of ajna chakra.

Almonds nourish our body, mind and spiritual abilities. They are high in protein and nutrients including calcium, zinc, magnesium, iron, potassium and vitamin E. Almonds provide all the vitamins and minerals needed for a strong healthy body and mind. They are the best nut for alkalizing the body. Soak your almonds overnight and peel the skin off, this improves digestibility.

Mantra: AUM - is the vibration of the supreme, representing the whole of Creation. Aum stimulates the entire spine and activates all the chakras. It also stimulates intuition and psychic awareness.

At ajna chakra we experience knowledge and mysticism but we are not yet fully united to the whole. Maya (illusions) can pull our consciousness back down into the lower chakras lowering our vibrations. To stay in high vibrations, we must keep our thoughts pure by reading spiritual books, keeping good company and always acting from a place of love.

Colour & Crystal Therapy

Indigo amplifies the colour blue and has a sedating vibration with cooling and quietening properties.

The energy of indigo is more introverted than blue and its awareness is internal. The energy of indigo has a fast vibration and we can experience profound thoughts, insights and inspiration working with this colour. It is related to psychic abilities such as clairaudience, clairvoyance and clairsentience. Awareness of this colour stills the mind so we can tune into the more subtle vibrations. Indigo energy promotes listening and is ideal to use in meditation and spiritual practice.

The rays of indigo crystals emanate mystery, intuition and wisdom.

Sodalite is a calming stone that clears the mind and helps develop focus and logical thinking. It is good for boosting the immune system and balancing the metabolism. This is a great stone for absorbing radiation and electromagnetic smog.

Lapiz lazuli is great for releasing physical, mental, emotional and spiritual blockages. It's cooling and soothing properties calm the mind and soothes the nervous system. It is a good stone to use for meditation and to alleviate insomnia and depression.

Other crystals that balance and heal this chakra include; sodalite, lapis lazuli, flourite, azurite, angelite, barite, celestite.

Aromatherapy

Clary sage is the oil of clarity and clear seeing. It is a fantastic oil for the third eye chakra. Clary sage dispels darkness and lifts the veil of illusion, illuminating truth. It opens the creative channels and clears the mind so the Divine light of consciousness and inspiration can flow, bringing in new fresh ideas and possibilities. Clary sage is a gentle oil that creates a feeling of euphoria, encouraging spiritual vision and enhanced perceptions of the spiritual world.

Other essential oils that are good for ajna include; sandalwood, frankincense and copaiba.

Archangel Uriel: Warrior of Intuitive Wisdom

Archangel Uriel is here to help us on our ascension journey. He lifts the veil of illusion, shining a light to expose the darkness. Uriel's flaming sword can assist us to purify lower vibrational energies and transmute them into spiritual understanding. Archangel Uriel connects with our third eye chakra, guiding us to see things from a higher perspective. He assists our creative ideas, insights, alchemy, magic and Divine universal wisdom.

Sahasrara – Crown Chakra – Be – Divine Connection

Sahasrara, our seventh chakra, resonates with the colour violet and has the highest most subtle vibration. It is situated at the top of the head. The crown chakra transcends illusions and limitations, connecting us to higher states of consciousness and the Divine. Sahasrara is the seat of enlightenment and a profound knowingness to all that is. Once we reach this level, the seed of our soul has sprouted from its roots in the earth, and grown upward through the elements of water, fire, air, space and light, and now to the source of all - consciousness itself. When this chakra is balanced, we feel connected to our higher Self, inspired, liberated and connected to all that exists.

Symbol Meaning of Sahasrara

Sahasrara is a thousand petalled lotus flower, situated at the crown of the head. The petals depict the story of the lotus flower blooming from the mud and blossoming into a beautiful flower. It is symbolic of our own growth, and the development of human consciousness.

Anatomy & Physiology of Sahasrara

The crown chakra governs the nervous system and brain. The nerve plexus of sahasrara is the cerebral cortex pineal plexus which is situated in the region of the pineal gland and associated with the cerebrum.

The endocrine gland associated with sahasrara is the pineal gland, a master gland situated in the mid-brain behind the thalamus. The pineal gland is the connecting link between the physical and spiritual worlds. It is the highest and most powerful source of energy for us to awaken to, that initiates supernatural powers within us. The pineal gland secretes hormones to communicate to the rest of the endocrine system. One of its main functions is to secrete melatonin, which regulates our circadian rhythm and biological cycle. Melatonin is stimulated by darkness and inhibited by light.

Avoiding fluoride will help to decalcify the pineal gland and awaken to higher levels of truth. You can use fluoride-free toothpaste and only consume purified water.

Physical signs this chakra is out of balance include; poor balance, clumsiness, co-ordination difficulties and epilepsy.

Psychology of Sahasrara

Sahasrara is the energy centre of Divine connection and One consciousness. When awakened, we transcend the limitations of the human construct and realise our fullest potential within the multidimensional holographic Universe.

When out of balance we feel disconnected to Spirit and out of touch with reality. Psychologically, mental health conditions relate to an imbalance in this chakra including; confusion, dementia and lack of spiritual exploration.

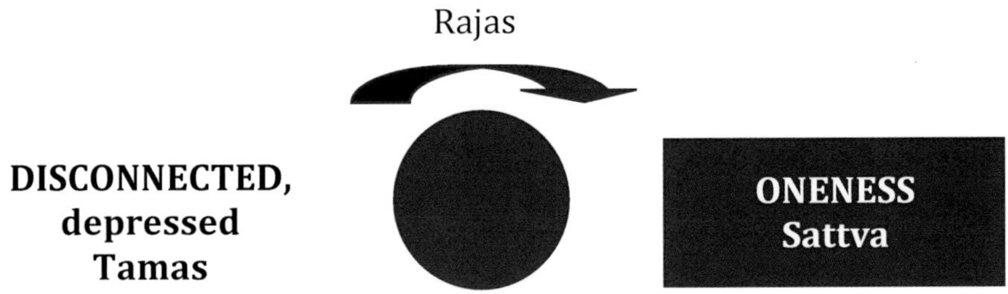

As the centre of enlightenment, sahasrara is naturally open to the cosmic life force energy. A person with a blocked crown chakra has cut off their connection to the Divine, ignorant to the Oneness of all; they are in a tamasic state spiritually. Through self-inquiry and devotion to sadhana, they initiate rajas and start to re-establish a relationship with themselves and their creator. With faith and a strong desire to evolve, sattva slowly increases, restoring their connection to the Divine and everything in creation.

An enlightened crown chakra develops when the sattvic level of awareness is maintained and there is no separation between the Self and the Divine. All is One. In this higher state of consciousness, all illusion dissolves and we come home to our eternal Self.

Balancing Sahasrara – Be – Divine Connection

To balance this chakra, feel the connection with universal consciousness and the One mind of all creation. Feel the power of the whole entire Universe where time and space cease to exist. Feel connected to everything around and within you. We are all connected to the interweaving web of consciousness. Feel that connection today as you go about your day.

Nutritional Therapy for Sahasrara

The best way to nourish sahasrara chakra is by fasting, meditation, devotion and prayer. The most profound and gratifying experience you will ever receive through fasting, prayer and meditation is Divine connection to Spirit and the entire cosmos.

We are going through a massive spiritual awakening, every day more and more people are waking up to the new Aquarian Age where love leads the way. We are already living in the 5th dimension.

We are moving away from the linear logical left brain thinking that is based around power and control, shifting consciousness into the feminine right brain of intuition and creativity.

MANTRA: AUM - The same mantra is chanted for the crown chakra as ajna, only now, we chant AUM silently.

<u>Colour & Crystal Therapy</u>

Violet is a soothing colour that increases the flow of imagination and spiritual energy. It sits at the opposite end of the spectrum to red and holds a combination of red and blue. The violet vibration transcends beyond the visible spectrum and is the door to the cosmic Universe and Heaven. Violet brings a new dynamic energy combing the heat of red with the cooling energy of blue. When these colours combine, they become very balancing for each other and bring about a sense of peace and serenity. The red tones ground the energies of the creative blue tones, balancing the life force energy. It is a great colour to use in meditation.

The energy of violet crystals contains the universal life force of magic, inspiration and destiny. They open your mind to higher states of consciousness.

Amethyst is a deeply spiritual crystal with a high vibration that transmutes negative energy into love. It is a great stone to use for meditation with its calming and balancing properties. It cleanses the aura, protects against psychic attack and opens the mind to other realities.

Labrodite raises consciousness and energises all of the chakras. It deflects negative energy and prevents positive energy from leaking out of the aura. It grounds spiritual energy into physical existence.

Other crystals that balance sahasrara include; diamond, moonstone, opal, quartz, selenite, phenacite, peacock ore and bismuth.

<u>Aromatherapy</u>

Roman chamomile is the oil of spiritual purpose. The calm, peaceful, uplifting energy of roman chamomile supports us on our spiritual journey. It guides us to follow our hearts and fulfil our life purpose. Other essential oils that are good for sahasrara include; frankincense and sandalwood.

<u>Archangel Zadkiel: Warrior of Illumination</u>

Archangel Zadkiel, whose name means 'Righteousness of God', teaches us to trust in the Divine omnipresent energy of creation. He brings about self-transformation and spiritual growth. Zadkiel is the Archangel of mercy, he encourages people to seek forgiveness, and helps us to forgive those who have hurt us.

Chakra Cleansing Practice

Take time every day to connect to each of your chakras, breathing light into each one. This can be done in a salt bath for ultimate indulgence and cleansing of the energetic body. Make sure to light some candles too!

Spend a minute or so breathing luminous white light into your base chakra, cleansing and balancing your energy. Once you feel ready, move onto the next one until you get all the way to the crown chakra. Then feel your whole body vibrating in white light, feeling the cleansing of your body, mind, heart and spirit.

Feel the light moving out into your aura, creating a bubble of energy around your entire being. Use this energy bubble of protection around you whenever you go outside. It will ward off negative vibes from other people and keep you in good spirits.

The Subtle Energy of Food

"Let food by thy medicine and medicine by thy food"
Hippocrates

Mother Nature provides us with all the medicine we will ever need. All the foods we consume have the potential to balance our body and mind, or cause disease to our system.

The foods we eat provide three levels of nutrition; the physical (5 elements), mental (sensory and mental impressions that we take in while we are eating) and spiritual (3 gunas) which are reflected in the other 2 levels. When we eat, our life force opens, and we are impressionable to our surroundings. Following a sattvic (pure) diet keeps our minds healthy, happy and peaceful.

Each day on this cleanse, you will connect with the medicine of food and listen to your body and its response to what you consume.

Whatever you choose to put into your body will have a direct impact on how you think and feel. High vibration foods will give you an abundance of energy and life force to live your life optimally. However, if you choose low vibration foods, your energy levels will be compromised and you will feel depleted and lethargic. Over time, continuing to over-consume all the wrong foods will inevitably disrupt the natural workings of the body and you will suffer in one way or another.

High Vibration Foods vs. Low Vibration Foods

What is the difference?

The energy in food vibrates at different frequencies depending on the quality of the food and where it was grown or manufactured.

Some people vibrate on a higher frequency than others. These kinds of people have a nutritious and balanced diet, think positive thoughts and have a positive outlook towards life. When we are aligned with our highest vibration, we are living our truth and are able to see and think more clearly. We have more positive and powerful thoughts going through our heads and we attract positive people and events into our lives. Our energy levels soar and we feel much happier.

High Vibration Foods

Foods grown in a natural environment with plenty of sunshine and pure water are considered high energy foods that contain an abundance of life force (prana) within them. We take nourishment from these nutrient-dense super foods, they provide us with optimum energy levels and great health. When we eat foods that vibrate at a higher frequency, we heighten our life force and become radiant and full of life.

Fruits that are grown on trees closest to the sun have the highest vibration as they contain the most sunlight. Include plenty of the following fruits in your diet; apples, pears, bananas, coconuts, mangos, lemons, limes, oranges, nectarines, plums, peaches, avocados, apricots, pomegranates, blueberries, cherries and olives. You can enjoy fruits freshly picked or make yourself a fresh juice to hydrate and oxygenate your cells and every system in the body.

Dark green leafy vegetables have a high vibration as they contain a high amount of chlorophyll, which absorbs sunlight. Make sure you eat plenty of organic spinach, kale, chard, Brussels sprouts, courgette, broccoli and bok choy. These greens also alkalize your system to balance its acidity, cleansing the entire system and removing toxins from the bloodstream. All other vegetables that are grown locally and organically in nutritionally balanced soil without pesticides contain a high vibration, so vary the vegetables you eat. I like to include all colours of the rainbow on my plate!

It is too easy to buy anything you desire these days due to improved packaging and transportation methods worldwide. Often these food products are depleted of vital nutrients and laced in chemicals to preserve them during shipping. Make sure you eat foods that are in season and produced locally to stay in balance with nature.

Nuts have a high vibrational frequency especially almonds, cashews, brazils, hazelnuts, macadamias, pecans, pine nuts, pistachios and walnuts that are grown on trees. Almonds contain the richest source of health-benefiting nutrients essential for optimum health. Aim to have a dozen almonds a day, soaked overnight and peeled. Seeds also contain natural energy; aim to include different types of seeds into your diet every day such as chia, hemp, pumpkin, sesame, sunflower and linseeds (flaxseeds).

Cacao (raw chocolate) contains an abundance of feel good phytonutrients, including anandamide, also known as the bliss molecule. Cacao heals the heart chakra and is a top source of antioxidants, vitamins and minerals, including magnesium, iron, potassium, phosphorus, manganese, tryptophan, zinc and copper.

Low Vibration Foods

Unhealthy foods lower your vibrations, making you vulnerable to sickness and disease. You should avoid all foods that are processed, preserved, refined, enhanced or genetically modified in any way. Foods which have a low vibration include meat, dairy products, canned, packaged, shelved and frozen products such as ready-made meals, cereals, soft drinks, alcohol, candy, cakes, biscuits, crisps etc.... Fast foods are also low vibration foods that contain little or no nutritional value.

How food is prepared and served also influences energetic frequencies. We consume the mental and emotional energies of the people who prepare our food which can have a detrimental or beneficial impact on our state of health. A loving meal made by a family member will have a much higher vibration than food prepared from a fast food establishment by someone who hates their job. When a meal is made with love and gratitude, the life force increases and you can feel the difference when eating the food.

Incorporate high vibration foods into your life today and watch your energy levels soar. Aim to eat a balance of colours from the rainbow when preparing your meals. This will help to balance your chakras and give you an abundance of energy.

What is Ayurveda?

Ayurveda means 'science and wisdom of life'. Ayurveda is the traditional Hindu system of medicine that dates back over 5,000 years. The ancient philosophy of Ayurveda is based on a deep understanding of the body, mind and spirit in relation to living in balance and harmony with Mother Nature, the seasons and our environment. Ayurveda is the sister science of yoga. It provides us with tools which we can apply to every aspect of our lives to maintain optimal health and wellbeing.

Ayurveda uses diet, lifestyle, herbs and body work to heal the mind-body and to prevent illness and disease. It is one of the most powerful treatments that provides healing at the root cause level. It works on the gross and subtle bodies. When we treat the subtle layers of our existence, it has a positive effect on the gross layers, changing the physical structures and allowing healing to occur.

Ayurveda is based upon the principles of the 5 elements; earth, water, fire, air and ether (space). Everything in the Universe is made up from these basic elements; they are the building blocks of life itself. Each of the elements makes up the biological elements (doshas) of our body and mind.

The 3 Doshas

The 3 biological elements; vata, pitta and kapha are dynamic forces of energy. Every person is unique depending on their individual constitution of each of these energies, also known as doshas. The characteristics of these doshas define our individual physical, mental and spiritual Self.

Vata is made up of space and air and is the energy of movement. It is very light, dry and cool. Vata controls bodily functions such as circulation, respiration and movement. It directs the other two doshas around the body just like the wind blows leaves through the sky.

Vata-dominant people tend to be slim, with prominent bones, and generally find it difficult to gain weight. Their minds are often busy, constantly jumping from one thought to the next. Worry and anxiety are signs this dosha can be out of balance. If you develop an excess of vata in your system, it is important to use opposite qualities to bring the mind-body back into balance. This person's diet should be warm, grounding and nutritious. Include foods which are sweet, sour and salty to balance the bitter, astringent and pungent qualities of vata. Avoid cold food and drinks. Warm food and drinks will balance vata.

Pitta is made up of fire and water and transforms matter into energy. It is hot, fiery and intense. Pitta controls temperature, metabolism and digestion. It is our inner fire where we burn our negative energy and transform it into positive energy. Pitta people tend to be of a muscular build and do not gain or lose weight easily. Their minds are focused and they make good leaders. Anger and irritation are signs this dosha is out of balance. The qualities of Pitta are pungent, salty and sour. If you develop an excess of pitta in your system, it is important to use the opposite qualities of sweet, bitter and astringent to bring your mind-body back into balance. Avoid hot spicy food. Cool foods and drinks will help to balance excess pitta.

Kapha is made up of earth and water and governs the structure of the body. It is heavy, solid and slow. Kapha controls weight, growth and formation of all tissues. It also provides structure in which the other 2 doshas move and flow throughout the body. Kapha people tend to have a bigger frame and can be prone to being overweight, they find it difficult to shift excess weight. They are loving, calm and patient with a tendency to become lazy and unmotivated. Insecurity and envy are signs this dosha may be out of balance. The qualities of kapha are sweet, sour and salty. If you have an excess of kapha in your system, it is important to use the opposite qualities; pungent, bitter and astringent to bring the body and mind back into balance. Avoid sweet and heavy foods. Spices are good for reducing an excess of kapha.

Vata-Pitta-Kapha is present in all organisms, every cell, tissue and organ. They create health when they are in balance and disease when out of balance. They are responsible for our genetic make-up and 1 or 2 of them are usually more dominant. There are 7 possible combinations of constitutions:

Vata
Pitta
Kapha
Vata - Pitta
Vata - Kapha
Pitta - Kapha
Vata - Pitta - Kapha (Tridosha)

We all have a pre-determined balance of the 3 biological elements vata, pitta and kapha. Your unique constitution of these 3 doshas is called your 'prakruti nature'. You are born with your unique prakruti and it never changes throughout your life (unless you are born again spiritually). When these qualities are balanced, you have a healthy body and mind. If any of your doshas were to increase due to conditions such as the weather, seasons, stress or dietary choices, then you would be in a state of imbalance. This is known as your 'vikrati'. If this is the case you need to change your lifestyle to recreate balance for your mind, body and spirit. Ayurveda seeks to restore health and balance our lifestyles, leading us to wellbeing and longevity.

Ayurveda & the Seasons

Once you know your unique mind-body type, it is possible to avoid illness and maintain optimal health and wellbeing all year round. Ayurveda teaches us how to live in harmony with the changes that are constantly occurring around and within us. For example, eating cooling foods in summer time to balance pitta; and reducing heavy foods in spring time to balance kapha. When we understand how the doshas flow with the tides of nature, we can stay balanced by adapting our diets and lifestyle. Kapha season is when it is cold and wet, during late winter through to early spring. Pitta season is summer time or when it is hot, and vata season is when it is cold and windy during autumn and early winter.

The 3 Gunas

In Ayurveda there are three primal forces of nature; sattva, rajas and tamas. These three gunas are subtle qualities of nature that form the foundations of life and our minds. They exist at a much deeper level than the three doshas. Our natural state is sattva.

Sattva is the quality of purity, intelligence and balance; providing us with clarity, happiness and inner peace. It is an upward moving energy leading us to enlightenment and liberation.

Rajas represents energy, activity and change. Too much rajas creates turbulence in our lives and the desire to always want more of the things that we think make us happy, but inevitably make us feel less than fulfilled.

Tamas is the quality of inertia, darkness and substance, which possess downward motion energy, holding things in limited material forms. When we focus only on the physical body, we remain in darkness and tamas prevails. People with psychological disorders are generally tamasic in nature and their energy tends to be stagnant and depleted.

Our aim is to live a sattvic lifestyle which enables us to remain balanced and in harmony with the world around us, completely in touch with our Divine spiritual nature. Sattvic foods such as basmati rice and fruits balance our mind-body while rajasic food like strong spices are stimulating, and tamasic foods including all processed, packaged and frozen foods are dull and life-less.

Too much rajas and tamas can create disharmony in our body and mind and cause disease. The more we increase sattva into our lives, the rajas and tamas energies balance out. Living a sattvic lifestyle creates balance and harmony within our mind-body connection, nature and Mother Earth.

The 6 Tastes and Their Elements

Sweet is made up of earth and water
Sour is made up of earth and fire
Salty is made up of water and fire
Bitter is made up of air and ether
Astringent is made up of earth and air
Pungent is made up of fire and air

The sweet taste is sattvic and harmonising to the mind-body, it is considered to be the primary taste. The energy of love is reflected in the sweet taste, a lack of love often leads to over-indulgence, eating too many sweet foods.

Rajasic tastes stimulate the senses and can irritate the mind-body. These tastes are sour, salty and pungent.

Tamasic tastes deplete our vital fluids when over consumed and include bitter and astringent tastes.

Our goal is to balance all six tastes at every meal and follow guidance for our unique mind-body type. By eating a sattvic diet in accordance with your constitution, your health and wellbeing will increase exponentially.

Agni: Our Internal Flame/Inner Fire

Agni, also referred to as the digestive fire, is essentially the health of your digestive system and ability to properly digest food. Digestion begins in the mouth; therefore, aiming to chew your food properly will help the stomach to stimulate the specific digestive juices needed to break down the different food groups.

Overeating, and making bad food choices and wrong food combinations can deplete your agni. Drinking cold drinks or finishing your meal with cold snacks or deserts such as ice cream can also extinguish agni, making you more susceptible to ama accumulation.

Ama is the build-up of toxins in the system and is the foundation of ill health. This build-up of ama and toxicity will spread throughout the body if left undealt with, which can affect the 7 types of tissues (plasma, blood, muscle, fat, bone marrow, nerve and reproductive) having a negative impact on all bodily systems such as digestive, lymphatic, respiratory and circulatory. This can affect the prana moving around within the body, depleting the subtle life force energy. If prana does not flow properly, the energetic body is also affected along with the mind. When this happens, you may experience negative thoughts, lack of focus, feel pessimistic, have a restless overactive mind, disturbed sleep, trouble concentrating and unhealthy cravings or addictions.

Vata types can be prone to irregular digestion with the wind and air fanning the digestive flame, allowing it to flicker and burn irregularly. This can lead to erratic eating patterns and appetite, gas, bloating, and indigestion issues.

Pitta types naturally have the strongest agni and digestion, which can lead to the 'eat whatever I want' mentality. Pitta have a strong fire element so the flame can burn strong and bright, but if it gets too strong, they can be likely to get out of balance, especially during warmer climates or when eating unsuitable foods, such as hot spices which would further increase their fire. As a result, heartburn, diarrhoea and excess acidity may develop.

Kapha types can be prone to suffering from the weakest agni as the cold dampness means the fire struggles to burn. Having a low agni can mean slower digestion or an inability to properly digest certain food groups, making it easier for ama to form. This can lead to a slower metabolism, weight gain and build-up of mucus and congestion, especially during cold and wet climates, which is kapha season.

Mindful Eating

Mindful eating enhances the nutritional properties of food. The food we choose to take in mindfully has the highest source of prana that sustains our physical, mental and psychic bodies.

Always eat in a relaxed and peaceful state of mind and environment. Even healthy foods can have negative impressions on your energetic body if eaten while you are in a bad mood. The energy of your negative thoughts and feelings store up in the body with the food that you eat, affecting all layers of your being. This energy penetrates you and affects the people you interact with; they too pick up on your negative vibrations. Shake off your negativity before eating, and only eat when you are in the right frame of mind.

Always bless your food and give thanks for the nourishment you receive from it. When you infuse your food with love, it opens up and gives you all its etheric treasures and purest most subtle energies.

Eating your meals in silence will create a calm and peaceful state of mind that will stay with you all day. Aim to chew your food at least 32 times to really break down the solid particles so they can be easily digested in the stomach. Concentrate on the food you are eating and do not let negative thoughts enter your mind. When you eat your meals in silence, consume the food whilst holding elevated thoughts and feelings so the experience becomes a spiritual practice that fuels your subtle bodies. Feel the magic in the silence of your meal times and draw the powerful etheric elements from it.

When we eat our meals, we don't just get nourishment from the physical aspects of the food. The colour, scent and sound all nourish our subtle bodies. They also nourish entities of the invisible world, and these Spirits are attracted to the kind of food we put into our bodies. Not only do we become what we eat, we also attract light benevolent beings or dark maleficent entities from the Spirit realm depending on the quality of the food we consume. This is the same for our thoughts and feelings. Our thoughts and feelings are the raw materials that form our subtle bodies. Positive thoughts and feelings attract luminous energies and negative thoughts and feelings attract dark energies.

What kind of energy and beings do you want to attract? Light angelic beings that can enhance your healing energies, or dark energies that keep you stuck in fear, pain and suffering?

Always be mindful, especially during mealtimes. Your body is your temple, it is important to respect your Divine vessel and fuel it with the most loving and luminous energies.

Nutrition is not just consuming food. Nutrition applies to anything we put into our bodies. Our spiritual practice, meditation and prayers are all forms of nutrition. These are the highest and subtlest forms of nutrition that feed us with the elixir of life; the Divine connection. By seeking to only consume highly luminous energy, we realise the truth of our existence; Oneness.

How Much Food Should You Eat?

Eating mindfully and stopping when you are 80% full is one way to control the mind, senses and desires. When we eat too much food, we put a strain on our digestive system and this often results in imbalance and the manifestation of illness.

By eating to the point just before you feel full, your body seeks elements from higher regions to fill the rest of your appetite. These etheric elements are pure spiritual energy that gives you an abundance of energy so you feel full of vitality and ready for your daily activities.

How to Extract Maximum Life Force from Food

The fruit and vegetables we eat are enriched with solar energy. We must learn how to extract that solar energy and information so we can evolve as human beings and increase our life force.

The sun is the highest and most luminous form of nourishment we can obtain. Starting your day watching the sunrise and absorbing the rays of the sun will enhance your vitality, strengthen your mind, body and willpower, and open your heart to love and light bringing peace to your entire being. When taking the time to watch the sunrise, we consume prana directly from the suns' rays and this gives us enough power to sustain our energy throughout the entire day, providing we do it consciously and with intention. This is the best way to start your day when partaking in a fast or cleanse of any sort.

Vegetarian Diet

Ahimsa is the yoga practice of non-violence and kindness to all living things. Vegetarianism is a great way to practice ahimsa and respect all living things as equal. Being vegetarian not only improves your health and extends your life, it contributes to saving our planet and natural resources - and our animals who, just like us, deserve to live a free and happy life.

Fruit and vegetables are a condensed form of light that nourish us on every level. There is not much sunlight in meat, it is dead energy and rots quickly in the body. This is hazardous to health.

When you eat meat, you are taking on the pain and suffering of the animal before and during its death. Animals have consciousness and are aware of their surroundings; they know when they are on their way to the slaughterhouse to be murdered. Once they sense this, fear rushes throughout their entire system and is trapped in their muscles as they die. By eating meat, you are taking on the fear and stress of that animal and it will have an impact on your system, lowering your vibrations and possibly stimulating anger and aggressive behaviour in your actions. On the astral plane this attracts lower entities that prey on fear and seek to find nourishment from people that vibrate on a lower frequency.

Apart from the ethical reasons as to why we should not eat animals, have you ever considered what happens to your insides when you eat meat? You no longer have a beautiful temple where your soul can dwell, you have replaced it with a graveyard full of dead animal corpses and have dead flesh rotting away in your digestive system, clogging up your energetic pathways and burdening your body.

I noticed a huge difference in my energy after giving up meat in my diet. My body and mind feel pure and I feel more compassion in my heart. Becoming vegetarian has changed my life in many ways; I feel healthier, lighter and more vibrant as a result.

Benefits of Cleansing

Cleansing is a great way to flush toxins and impurities from your system. You will notice an increase in energy levels, mental focus, clarity, confidence, self-discipline and overall sense of wellbeing.

Cleansing strengthens the immune system, boosts metabolism and rids the body of excess fat. It reduces stress levels, pain and inflammation, initiating healing within the body. Your appearance will be more youthful and radiant when you continue to rejuvenate your body and mind with regular cleansing.

Cleansing leaves you feeling vibrant, with a zest for life!

During a cleanse or fast, the body is relieved the burden of digesting food. Instead, the energy is used to break down the undigested food in the digestive system, releasing toxic build up. There is more energy available to supply fresh oxygenated blood to all the systems of the body, improving their functioning. The body is encouraged to eliminate waste and to heal itself.

It is advised to do a 24-hour cleanse or fast once a week or 2-3 days once a month.

The Wonderful Benefits of Fasting

All food, even pure food, leaves waste in our bodies and can accumulate in the tissues and organs. Quite often people think of fasting as depriving the body. This is far from true. The main purpose of fasting is purification and nourishing the spirit. Once you stop feeding food to the physical body, the etheric and astral bodies work more actively to draw in spiritual energy from higher sources. This increases the strength of our light body and is enlightening for our soul. Fasting is a period of abstinence from all food or specific items. Fluids are consumed in sufficient quantities to satisfy thirst and physiological requirements.

Fasting improves the system's immunity and brings about a rapid detoxification of the body. Sometimes dry fasts are practised as part of spiritual activities and worship. This kind of fast is amazing for awakening your higher Self to the Universe and feeling the Divine cosmic energy penetrate your entire being. During a dry fast you abstain from food and water. Your source of prana is derived directly from Spirit. You will feel light, revitalised, rejuvenated and have an abundance of energy when you purify your systems through fasting. You will sleep better, have a stronger resistance to disease and feel creative with lots of new ideas. Your senses will be much sharper and you will hear the voice of your angels easier.

When taking part in a fast, I like to think of it as taking time out for myself. Plan some pampering sessions, go for a massage, have a relaxing Epsom salt bath with aromatherapy and candles, play soothing music. Go for a walk, give yourself a foot soak and pedicure, or get lost in a good book. There are so many things you can do to make yourself feel good without even touching food. Let's look at some of the benefits of fasting, and guidelines on how to fast safely for your unique body-mind type. One thing is for sure, prayer is an essential component in fasting, especially if you are embarking on more than a 24 hour fast, as you will transcend the body and mind and rely on spiritual energy to sustain you.

The Healing Power of Fasting

Eating food excessively on a continuous basis creates a burden for the body. Your stomach is roughly the size of your fist therefore when you do eat you should eat smaller portions of food so the body can easily digest it. The body and mind will suffer when the stomach is forced to handle more than it is comfortable with. During fasting, we rest our system from the constant onslaught of food. A lot of energy is required to digest, assimilate and metabolize our food, so when we stop eating, the energy is redirected to healing and repairing bodily systems. The body can concentrate on eliminating toxins and fat cells from the body instead of working on digestion. Fasting is a popular treatment to cure many diseases and can show us our weak spots in the body, indicating where to change our lifestyle and take precautions to prevent illness and disease from manifesting. When combined with yoga, fasting can quickly improve many conditions. By eliminating obstructions, cleansing and purifying the intestines, blood and the cells, we can overcome many of our physical illnesses as well as getting a boost in energy levels. The therapeutic use of fasting will allow the body to use excess energy to speed up the healing process of disease.

Fasting not only removes obstructions and helps the body to heal from within, it is also rejuvenating and life extending. These resulting benefits can have lasting effects in your mental and emotional health. Fasting is a great way to release emotional patterns, promoting greater mental clarity and inner stillness, enhancing our spiritual connection.

Our bodies know how to heal themselves naturally, so it is important for us to get out of our own way and allow the body to rebalance physically, mentally, emotionally and spiritually. Some of the physical health benefits to fasting include reducing the risk of cancer, diabetes, insulin resistance, cardiovascular disease and immune disorders.

The Physiology of Fasting

Glucose is the body's primary fuel source and it is essential for the body and brain's functioning. When denied glucose for more than 6-8 hours, the body turns to the liver for glycogen, a storage form of glucose, to be used for fuel. Glycogenolysis converts glycogen into a usable form of fuel. Small amounts of protein are also used at this point to supplement the fuel, which will last up to 12 hours before the body needs to turn to glycogen stored in the muscles, lasting a few more days. If glucose is still denied, muscle wasting is prevented by temporarily switching to fat as the fuel source, meaning that fat is converted to ketone bodies through catabolism. The body continues to use fat for as long as there is fat to consume.

Fasting & Weight Loss

Weight loss is a natural by-product of fasting however, I wouldn't recommend taking part in a fast to solely lose weight. Fasting is a way to improve your health and wellbeing and is great for changing your mindset and thought processes around food. It will give you a new perspective on your relationship with food and help you to release emotional attachments, shifting your mentality to make lasting changes to your diet and lifestyle.

Your body will become more sensitive to certain foods once you break your eating cycle, then when you re-introduce different food types back in to your diet gradually, you will notice what feels good for you and what your body doesn't like. Learn to listen to your body's natural rhythms, and trust your intuition when considering your choices. Food is energy for us, not just something we consume for pleasure. By thinking about the affect the food will create in your body and mind, you will become more mindful and want to nourish your body with healthy foods that will leave you feeling vibrant and full of life.

Emotional & Mental Benefits of Fasting

When considering a fast you must ensure you are in the right frame of mind. This will determine your success. You will need to maintain a positive mental attitude and work through any issues that may present themselves during this process. Keeping a journal will help you to stay focused and on the right track as you will see exactly what you are eating, and you can bring your attention to why you eat the way you do. Are you eating because you are really hungry? Or are you bored, stressed and eating to hide or supress your feelings? Are you eating the wrong types of food in a belief that nutritious alternatives are too time-consuming to prepare?

A lot of the time emotional hunger is confused with physical hunger. Sometimes we use food as a substitute for what we are lacking in our lives such as love and affection. Fasting helps us to address our emotions and to deal with them.

Emotionally, you will feel much happier and calmer, with improved concentration, less anxiety and better sleep patterns. I love how refreshed I feel when I wake up after a fast; it is very uplifting.

Mental clarity and focus are both improved during fasting. It can become a tool in your life to give you clearer perspective, greater freedom, flexibility, and energy to get things done.

Spiritual Benefits of Fasting

When we fast, the body becomes lighter and less dense. This creates a subtle separation from ordinary physical reality, and you begin to sense the presence and power of the things we cannot see in this physical world. Our minds redirect inward and we become quiet, where quality time can be spent connecting to your higher Self and Spirit. It is easier to attain higher states of consciousness and the messages and guidance from your Spirit guides will be much clearer and easier to hear. You realise that we are all here on Earth with a life purpose and you will intuitively reconnect to the Divine plan and know that you are guided by a force that is beyond intellectual comprehension. Listen to your intuition and pay attention to the little things. You will notice Divine synchronicities that will guide you along your journey, confirming that you are on the right path. I love the deeper connection you feel to Spirit when fasting. Anything I asked for during the Sun Moon Dance in Scotland where I dry fasted for 4 days, Spirit delivered without fail. My Spirit and faith were put to the test and I was strong enough to transcend body, mind and emotions. For this, all my needs were met.

Fasting & the Doshas

Fasting is great for kapha individuals. Considering you are fit and well, a fast for a kapha dominant person could last for 3 days quite easily without any implications.

Pitta individuals do well on a fast but should limit to a maximum of 36 hours. For instance, you could eat at breakfast or lunch time on day one, and then break your fast the following evening at dinner time.

Vata dominant people have to be the most careful when embarking on a fast. Their light and airy nature can become out of balance quite easily when they don't eat often and they should only fast for up to 24 hours. It is best to have dinner at 6pm on day one, then break the fast the following day at the same time or earlier if needed.

The art of fasting is about tuning into your mind-body and learning what works best for you. I love fasting and practice it often as part of my sadhana. My prakriti is pitta-vata therefore in summer I generally fast for up to 36 hours and in winter when it is cold it is best not to fast, however I often feel guided by Spirit to include fasting as part of my regular routine and tend to do just 24 hours in accordance to my vata dosha.

Only take part in fasting if it is something you feel drawn to on a spiritual level and you are ready to transform your life in spectacular ways.

<u>When to do a Fast</u>

A fast works best in warm weather. In the colder seasons, the body requires food for energy to increase the core temperature of the body. A general fast can last from 1 day to 3 days unsupervised. During this time the body has sufficient time to cleanse and give the whole system a rest.

You should also keep the mind active during a fast and try not to think about food. If your cravings become excessive you should stop the fast.

The most important aspect of fasting is breaking the fast. To break a fast, you will need to wean your body back on to solid food just like you would wean a baby onto food. Therefore, consume liquids for the next 24 hours or break your fast with a fresh piece of juicy melon. You can then gradually introduce solid foods.

After the fast your stomach will have shrunk and will require less food, so make sure you do not over-eat. Feed your body well. Listen to your body; stop eating when you are full. Drink plenty of water. A lot of the time when we think we are hungry we are actually thirsty. When you think you are hungry have a glass of water and wait 30 minutes, if you are still hungry then have something to eat.

Avoid strenuous exercise for a few days. Yoga is recommended to build energy and cleanse all your bodily systems. When I dry fast at the Sun Moon Dance, my yoga practice is just as strong on day 4 as it is on day 1, in fact I feel stronger, more flexible and lighter by the end of the dance. It is amazing how much physical and mental strength you acquire when abstaining from food and water. You truly do transcend all limitations of the body, mind and emotions. I feel a deeper sense of profound clarity that cannot be described in words.

If you struggle to do a full fast, alternatively, try a mono fast. A mono fast consists of eating only 1 thing throughout the day; i.e. apples or pears work the best. Stewed fruit is best for vata and kapha, raw for pitta.

<u>How to Fast</u>

You can fast in many ways, I recommend you try intermittent fasting first to see how you manage, not just physically but mentally and emotionally too. Try eating in an 8-hour window, say 10am - 6pm and fast for a 16-hour period. When you don't eat for long periods of time, your body uses fat as fuel instead of carbohydrates, turning you into a lean fat burning and healing machine.

While fasting, the body is highly conservative of its energy and resources. It allows a deep, physiological rest of the digestive organs and the energy saved goes into self-healing and self-repairing.

When we fast, we derive energy from a higher source and tap into the Divine spiritual energy of the cosmos. It truly is a liberating experience. During the 8-hour window frame eat an abundance of fruit, vegetables, pulses, legumes, beans, nuts and seeds, and drink plenty of water. It is important to consume food with high life force to replenish your cells and maximize your energy.

When we fast, our main source of nourishment comes from air instead of food, so it is important to include time in nature as part of your day.

Side Effects of Detoxification & Fasting

During a 24-hour detox it is common to suffer with a headache. The severity will depend on your diet before you commenced the plan. If you usually consume high amounts of caffeine then the headache will be worse due to the caffeine withdrawal. To prevent this, cut back on caffeine before your cleanse, making sure you drink plenty of water. The headache should eventually subside. You can also practice deep breathing and meditation to help control the headache.

When you undertake a longer detox, toxins will be released from your body and it is common to suffer with bad breath, sweating and tremors. This is a natural process and will soon disappear.

The symptoms and side effects we may experience during a fast indicate weaker areas in the body. This is nature's way of communicating with us, warning us that we may suffer in these particular areas in the future. This knowledge enables us to take better care of ourselves and the particular areas that are causing distress and pain. All the symptoms we experience are a result of the cleansing effects that occur as the toxic waste enters the bloodstream to be eliminated. Know that this process is natural and allow your body to naturally release the built-up toxins.

Drinking plenty of hot lemon water will help to cleanse the channels of the body and remove impurities. Stay positive during your cleanse and know that these symptoms will pass once the toxins have been eliminated. It may be best to consult your doctor before starting your cleanse, especially if you are on any medication or concerned in any way.

Preparing to do a Fast

To begin a fast, you need to prepare yourself mentally and physically. You should only take part in a fast when you feel ready in body and mind. When preparing to do a fast you need to cut out red meat, dairy products, grains which contain gluten (wheat, rye, barley, oats), sugar, sucrose, glucose, alcohol, caffeine and condiments such as mayonnaise, tomato sauce etc.

Depending on your unique mind-body type, try to consume raw food as much as possible, as it contains more nutrients and fibre, and cleans the gut more efficiently. Raw foods are much harder to digest and are therefore not suitable for everyone. Pitta dominant people thrive off raw food. Vata and Kapha should incorporate room temperature vegetables and fruit, and consume with a warm ginger tea to help with digestion.

For maximum cleansing and vitality, include the following foods into your diet before and after a cleanse or fast. These foods are sattvic in nature and the best food choices for living an Ayurvedic yoga lifestyle:

Vegetables - High in fibre, vitamins and minerals
Fruit - High in fibre, vitamins and minerals
Pulses and legumes - High in nutrients and protein
Rice - High in nutrients and fibre, easily digested and very filling
Herbs and spices - Healing properties and for flavour
Yoghurt - Coconut yoghurt, probiotic rich with good bacteria
Milk and cheese - Soy, nut, rice and oat milks, vegan cheese
Nuts - Essential fatty acids
Oils - Essential fatty acids

Start introducing more liquids into your diet prior to fasting. Juice and smoothies supply the body with essential vitamins and minerals, helping to cleanse and restore the body.

<u>The Benefits of Juicing</u>

Fresh, raw, unpreserved juices contain an abundance of amino acids, minerals, enzymes and vitamins that the body needs to nourish and regenerate cells, tissues, glands and organs, with minimum digestive effort. Fruit juices are the cleansers of the human system; vegetable juices are the builders and regenerators.

<u>What is the Difference Between a Juice & Smoothie?</u>

A juice extracts the raw vitamins and minerals from the food but leaves behind a lot of wastage. It is also stripped of fibre making it easier to digest. Someone who has low agni may find that juices are better for them as the digestion does not have to work as hard. It is advisable to add a little warm water and a bit of cinnamon or fresh ginger to the juice also to help aid digestion.

There is no wastage of food in smoothies, as all of the fruit and vegetables that go into the machine are incorporated into a smoothie and you drink the whole lot. The fibre is still intact and will leave you feeling fuller for longer.

Both fresh juice and smoothies are high in prana; the natural life force from the sun captured within the food. Where possible, try to buy locally grown produce, favouring organic goods to reduce exposure to pesticides and ensure the food is fresh and has not been sat around whilst being transported from the other side of the world.

Juices & Smoothies for Each of the Doshas

Putting your high prana foods into a blender is a great way to get a huge hit of nutrients straight into the blood-stream to nourish all of your systems. There are general rules for each of the doshas when it comes to food and drink, and the following guidelines will help you understand your mind-body to ensure you make the right nutritional choices around your juices and smoothies.

Pitta individuals are most suited to cold or cooler foods, especially in summer when the weather is hot. Having a strong digestion with the fire element being dominant, these kinds of people thrive off raw food, juicing and smoothies. Favour sweet, bitter and astringent tastes and add mint for extra cooling properties.

Vata and kapha are better suited to warmer foods all year round. This doesn't mean avoiding juices or smoothies, but add room temperature water to them to help digestion. Make sure you keep your fruit and vegetables at room temperature before putting them through the blender. Spices such as cumin, coriander, fennel, cardamom, ginger and mint can be added to help with digestion.

Vata do well with fresh sweet fruit juice and smoothies, which can be a great snack between meals, whilst kapha are best suited to the lighter green variations to help with cleansing and removing excess build-up of ama within the body. For kapha, it is great to have these as a meal replacement, especially if you are trying to lose weight.

Kitcheri: The Ayurvedic Superfood

Kitcheri is a yogi superfood and a traditional Ayurvedic dish that is known for its cleansing and healing properties. It is the basic staple for a yogic diet. My ultimate favourite is pineapple kitcheri which was inspired by one of my favourite dishes in Thailand, pineapple rice. Kitcheri is a complete protein, contains lots of vitamins, minerals and antioxidants and is completely delicious! The three main ingredients are rice, mung beans and ghee.

Although ghee has many health benefits, the Chakra Yoga Cleanse is a vegan plan, so we are substituting ghee with coconut oil.

Rice is the king of all grains in Ayurveda

White basmati rice is the best option. It is light, easily digested and packed full of nutrients. It is also low in fat and an excellent source of carbohydrates. Basmati rice provides the body with key nutrients such as iron, manganese and B vitamins. On the Glycaemic Index, basmati rice and brown rice both have a medium G.I. White basmati rice is the better choice when making this dish for a cleanse, as it gives the digestive system a rest. If you are incorporating kitcheri into your healthy lifestyle, brown rice can also be used to increase fibre content.

Mung beans are a superfood and a nutritional powerhouse!

Mung beans are rich in protein, folic acid, iron, zinc, potassium, phosphorus, copper, magnesium, manganese, thiamine, and vitamin C. They are high in fibre, low in saturated fat and contain no cholesterol. All the nutrients in mung beans strengthen the immune system, metabolism and other organs in the body. The antioxidants in the mung beans protect us against free radicals and disease. Mung beans also contain anti-inflammatory, antifungal and antibacterial properties. The beans are easily digested and make this dish a complete protein.

Coconut oil contains healthy fatty acids that provide energy to the body and brain

Saturated fats are either long-chain, medium-chain or short-chain fatty acids. The long-chain fatty acids are dangerous to the body and are to be avoided in the diet. These types of saturated fat are found in most animal fat. Short-chain and medium-chain fatty acids are assimilated, absorbed and then metabolised into energy. The saturated fats in coconut oil are mainly medium chain triglycerides (MCT), which are anti-inflammatory, anti-microbial, anti-bacterial, anti-fungal, and have antioxidant properties. Rich in lauric acid, coconut oil enhances the immune system and can prevent infections and disease. MCT's also produce hormones that promote feelings of fullness, which will curb cravings and assist a healthy relationship with food.

When making kitcheri, the staple spices are asafoetida, cumin seeds and coriander. These herbs balance all three doshas. You can add other spices and vegetables to your kitcheri according to your constitution.

Good vegetables for vata include; asparagus, beets, carrots, parsnip, leeks, squash and sweet potato. Favour sweet, salty and sour tastes. Good vegetables for pitta include; asparagus, green beans, broccoli, sprouts, cabbage, cauliflower, celery, kale, leeks, mushrooms, squash and peas. Favour bitter, sweet and astringent tastes.

All vegetables are good for kapha, but reduce consumption of sweet and juicy vegetables such as sweet potatoes, corn, beets and courgettes. Favour bitter, pungent and astringent tastes.

The good thing about this dish it that is so versatile. You can change the vegetables each time to create a whole new meal. Play around to find out how you enjoy it most.

PART 2 – PRACTICAL

Chapter 5: Setting Up Your Sacred Space

Find a space for your practice and make sure it is clear and calm. Set up an altar to create the right ambience. On your altar, place something that symbolises each of the elements. As you will see above, I have crystals for the Earth, oils for the water element, candles for fire and feather for air. You can also light incense or a use a diffuser with the essential oils as recommended for each chakra.

I have created my own meditation blends for each of the chakras and also put crystals in them for amplification of energies. They are available for order and include a free consultation to tailor your bespoke blends for each of the chakras (details at the back of the book). You can also have some angel cards on the alter. Ask your angels for guidance upon commencing the cleanse and keep your messages on the altar to inspire and motivate you along your journey. At the start of every session, sit in front of your altar and spend a moment connecting with your heart. Tune into the Angelic Realms and open yourself to the limitless potential of the Universe. Smell your essential oils directly from the bottle, feeling the aroma open your energetic pathways infusing your body, mind and soul with the unique properties of the oils. Rub a little on your wrists and behind your ears so it can get into your bloodstream and start to work its magic.

Preparing for Your Practice

Each day on the Chakra Yoga Cleanse you will progress upwards through the chakras, building on the practice from the previous day.

For each chakra you have a seated and standing pose. As you move through the chakras, do all seated poses first and then the standing poses to build your practice. For example, on day 2, you will practice seated poses for day 1 and 2, then standing poses for day 1 and 2. On day 3, you will do seated poses for day 1, 2 and 3, then standing poses for day 1, 2 and 3. You will continue this all the way to day 7, where you will do all 7 seated poses for each of the charkas, and then all 7 standing poses for each of the chakras.

By the end of the week you will have developed a chakra yoga flow that can now be the foundation for your yoga practice moving forward. To deepen your yoga practice and learn more about the chakras, you can join my online Chakra Yoga Cleanse. All information is at the back of this book.

Depending on your current eating habits and whether you are used to fasting regularly already, you may want to modify the cleanse plan. You can follow the cleanse 100% or play around with creating your own based on the recipes provided.

For example, I often only have 2 meals a day and would choose to have a smoothie for breakfast around 10am then make a delicious pan of soup and have an early dinner around 4pm. The important thing is, that you have your morning juice/smoothie to start your day with a hit of nutrients and the bright colours of the chakra we are working with on that day. This can be at any time of the morning.

Another option would be to have the soup for lunch and dinner. This is a great time-saving option, plus, you get to enjoy that delicious soup you made twice in one day, bonus! The soup recipes are based on 2 servings so this would work really well if you are just cooking for yourself. Otherwise you can freeze your extra soup for the next week and take delight in another round of the chakra yoga cleanse.

Either way, the choice is yours. You have plenty of options. I have created this cleanse to introduce you to working with your chakras on a daily basis, and to build your spiritual toolbox to purify your system, restore balance to your light body and assist you on your transformational journey.

This is also an introduction to fasting and developing more control and discipline in your life.

Ultimately, discipline creates freedom and brings us great joy!

I am honoured to be your guide as we journey through the rainbow bridge to Heaven on Earth. Are you ready? Let's do this!

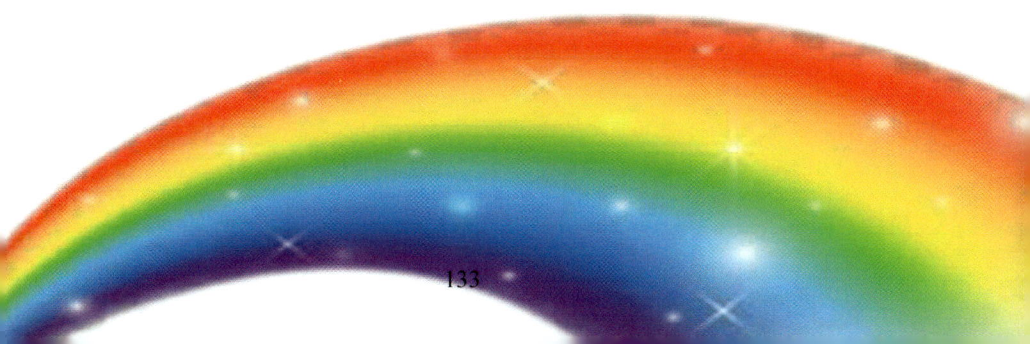

If you don't have a yoga mat, practicing on the carpet or a large towel is fine. Wear loose clothing, so you can move freely with ease.

It is best to do your yoga practice at the same time every day. On this cleanse you will be doing short morning and evening practices to get you into a healthy routine. Starting your day with yoga slowly wakes up the body and mind, easing you into the day ahead with peace and positivity. You will feel healthier and happier throughout the day when you make the effort to do yoga first thing. Once you start feeling the benefits of a regular morning practice you will feel motivated to continue, and even look forward to getting up each day with yoga on your mind.

<u>The Power of Intention</u>

To make lasting changes in your lifestyle and change the neural pathways in your mind-body connection, it is important to be consistent with intentions and thoughts.

We will always begin and end the yoga practice with the same intention, using a different theme each day. Repetition yields powerful results and the more you repeat your intentions and infuse them with the energy of Sanskrit mantra and chants, the stronger your mind-body and life force will be. The benefits of your morning practice will ripple through your entire day.

Power of the Pen – Keeping a Journal

A wonderful part of your journey on the Chakra Yoga Cleanse is to develop a daily writing habit. After your morning practice and before you go to bed at night, keep a journal to record your feelings and experiences during the cleanse. This is a great way to deal with issues that may arise for you, and will also help you to stay focused towards your goals.

Creating Healthy Habits

Healthy habits improve health, raise our vibrations, clear the energy field and boosts positivity. Life becomes effortless when we flow with the current of life rather than against it. Creating and maintain healthy habits is key for optimum health and wellbeing.

Morning routine

Upon waking: Scrape your tongue with a copper tongue scraper then oil pull using sesame or coconut oil. Swish ½ - 1 tbsp of oil in your mouth for 10 – 20 minutes gently pulling it in and out through your teeth. Spit it out into the garbage bin and rinse your mouth with salt water. Brush your teeth as normal. Once you have removed the toxins from your mouth, drink a glass of warm water to hydrate your system.

Yoga: Enjoy your yoga practice on an empty stomach before your breakfast.

Breakfast: Prepare and enjoy in a relaxed and calm state of mind.

Mid-morning: It is good to stretch throughout the day. I recommend you practice the top 3 poses for a healthy spine and digestion on day 3, every day mid-morning. Get into the habit of doing this short sequence each day to keep your spine and posture healthy. Then enjoy a piece of fruit the same colour as the chakra you are working on. Feel it nourishing that particular chakra as you connect with the subtle energies within the fruit.

Evening routine:

- Go for a short walk in nature after dinner if possible and focus on absorbing the life force from your surroundings.
- Spend time journaling to enhance your practice and journey.
- Do something relaxing such as giving yourself a massage or indulge in an aromatherapy bath with Epsom salts. Light some candles and listen to beautiful music.
- Have a relaxing herbal tea, such as chamomile or lavender.
- Practice your evening sadhana to help you relax your body and mind, preparing for a deep peaceful sleep.
- Get into a routine of going to bed before 10pm.

As I was writing one day, making a list of things you can do to raise your vibrations, all of a sudden, a star manifested and I knew the Angels created it through me! It is quite obvious when you look at the central line of the star diagram below that this is so. Make sure you are doing everything in this star to raise your vibrations and increase your health and wellbeing. Print a copy of the star and place it somewhere you will see it every single day. Take time to connect with your higher Self for guidance and support to include the following activities into your daily life:

^

Sing

Dance

Meditate

Practice yoga

Be more mindful

Eat highly nutritious foods

Be yourself and speak your truth

Drink plenty of water to stay hydrated

< Connect to your Spirit Guides and Angels >

Go for walks outdoors

Spend time in nature

Have a massage

Take time out

Sleep well

Laugh

v

Chapter 6: Chakra Yoga Cleanse

Gateway to Heaven on Earth

This 7-day chakra yoga cleanse will provide you with a strong foundation for developing a regular yoga practice and establishing healthy nutrition for your unique mind-body type.

Each day you will journey through the chakras, starting at the base of the spine at muladhara, travelling all the way to sahasrara at the crown of the head. By the end of the week, you will have a toolbox of techniques that you can use in your life to boost your energy levels, free up stagnant energies and let go of things that are no longer serving you.

The theme for each day will give you focus, enabling you to connect with the elements that make YOU the person you are.

Opening Your Yoga Practice

You can achieve anything you desire with the right intentions and mindset. An intention is a short powerful statement that affirms a goal you have set and intend to achieve. When you repeat your intentions, you plant new seeds in your subconscious mind. The more you nurture these seeds, the more you allow yourself to grow and evolve into a happier, healthier and more positive person. Any time a negative thought arises in your mind, replace it with your positive intentions. Implement your intentions regularly throughout the day and watch your life transform in incredible ways!

During this cleanse, you will have your own personal intentions of what you want to achieve. Powered with your daily theme, you will also have an affirmation to help strengthen each of your chakras to elevate your energy and consciousness.

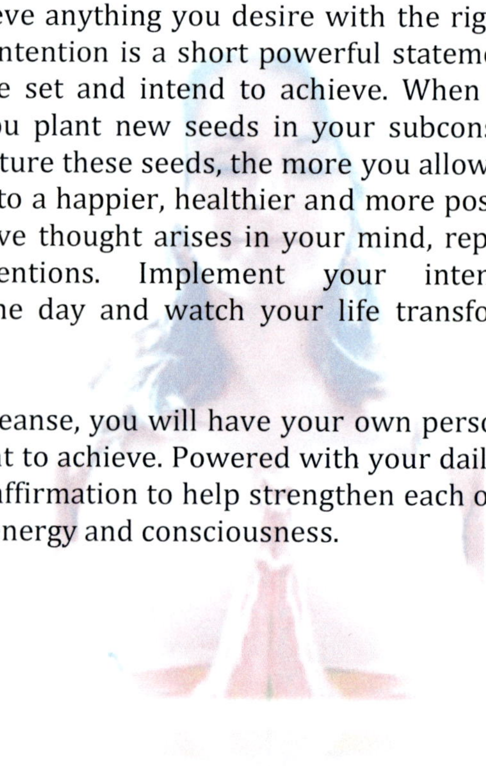

Day 1 – EARTH – Ground & Connect

"I am Strong, I am Grounded"

Sukhasana – Easy Seat Pose

When we wake up in the morning, it is important to connect with the Earth and make sure we are fully in our body, returned from dreamtime and the astral realm. Sukhasana balances the root chakra and your connection to the Earth and your physical body. It strengthens the back and spine, improves posture and is calming for the brain and mind.

Sit in a comfortable seated position with your legs crossed, or if you are sat on a chair both feet should be relaxed on the ground. Place your palms facing down on your knees. Lengthen through your spine and relax shoulders down away from the ears. Begin to notice the natural rhythm of your breath. Does your breathing feel slow or fast? Are you breathing shallow or deep?

Deep Abdominal Breathing

Place one hand on your chest and the other on your lower belly. Bring awareness to the rise and fall of your abdomen, breathing in and out through the nose. Inhale, feel the abdomen rise, chest expand and collar bones rise. Exhale and feel the whole body relax, letting go of any tension. Continue with deep abdominal breathing for a few minutes, observing the rise and fall of the abdomen with each breath.

Connecting with the Earth: Creating a Strong Foundation

Inhale, feel the breath moving all the way down into the pelvic floor. Visualise a red ball of energy glowing at the base of your spine. Exhale, visualise roots extending down from both sit bones growing deep down into the centre of the Earth, wrapping around the Earth's core grounding you into your physical body.

Mulabandha: Root Lock

Feel your roots strong and grounded. Inhale, feel the life force energy drawing up from the centre of the Earth, travelling all the way up your roots and into your sit bones. Notice that the glow of muladhara is shining vibrantly. As you exhale, slowly release the breath and gently contract your pelvic floor muscles to activate mulabandha and awaken the dormant life force potential of your kundalini energy. Inhale and breathe deep into your pelvic floor allowing all the muscles to relax. As you exhale, slowly release the breath, gently contract mulabandha, lift the lower belly, and draw your navel in towards your spine and up to the heart. Visualise the energy rising all the way up the spine towards the third eye.

Connect with the Heavens: Visualise Your Dreams

Visualise a bright white light flowing into your crown chakra, filling up your whole body with luminous energy.

Focus on your third eye and use your imagination to create a crystal clear image of what you want to achieve over the next 7 days. Throughout the cleanse, you will be re-directing your lower energies to this point of focus and concentration. Use your kundalini powers to break free from limiting beliefs and anything that may be holding you back.

Feel the energy flowing in through the crown chakra from the Heavenly Realms, infusing your vision with clarity. Once your vision is crystal clear, set your personal intention and repeat it 3 times, feeling it deep in your heart and soul, then affirm:

"I am Strong, I am Grounded"

Tadasana – Mountain Pose

Tadasana improves posture and is great for grounding the body and mind, setting a strong foundation for your practice.

Stand with your feet hip distance apart, arms relaxed by the sides of the body. Become aware of the contact points between your feet and the ground.

Pada Bandha – Foot lock

Pada bandha is key to maintaining stability in standing poses. Firmly press the balls of your feet into the earth and flex your toes up towards the shins. Feel the ball of the foot, the base of the little toe and the centre of the heel all connected to the Earth, and visualise a triangle forming from each of these points. As you engage these muscles of the feet by standing correctly, you should begin to feel the 3 arches in your foot. The medial longitudinal arch runs from the ball of the foot to the centre of the heel. The lateral longitudinal arch runs from the base of the little toe to the centre of the heel. The transverse arch runs across the foot from the base of the little toe to the ball of the foot.

Feel both feet strong and grounded as you connect to the Earth. Visualise roots extending down from each of these contact points growing deep into the Earth. As you inhale, visualise a red ball of life force energy coming all the way up through the Earth into your roots. Feel this energy moving into your feet, ankles, lower legs, knees, thighs and hips. Your legs are completely strong and grounded like a mountain, as you stand in this vibrant red ray of light.

Inhale the breath deeply and fully. Exhale, let your shoulders relax down and away from the ears, rolling the shoulders back slightly to open the chest and expand the heart. Turn your palms facing forwards. Stand here in mountain pose, tall and confident for a few minutes every morning. Activate mulabandha and feel the power that resides within you. Awaken your potential and step boldly into your day with positivity and greatness.

Throughout the day, be mindful of your posture, any time you feel yourself slouching bring awareness back to mountain pose and re-adjust your posture to bring balance back into both sides of the body and mind.

Muladhara Cleanse

Watermelon Juice

- ¼ watermelon

Chop up and blitz in a blender until smooth. Visualise the vibrant red juice energise and vitalise your root chakra. Feel the vibrant red colour flowing through your body all day long, nourishing you and giving you an abundance of energy.

Lunch - Stuffed Red Peppers with Quinoa Salad

- 1 large red pepper
- ¼ cup of quinoa
- 2 mushrooms
- 1 portobello mushroom
- ½ pomegranate
- ¼ litre of bouillon
- Coriander
- Asparagus
- Pecans
- Salt & pepper

Cook the quinoa in the bouillon for 20 minutes. Finely chop the mushrooms, add to the pan and cook for another few minutes.

Mindfully cut the lid off the pepper. Add the pomegranate and coriander to the quiona and mix well. Stuff half of the quinoa salad into the pepper and leave the other half in the pan with lid on to keep it warm. Put the stuffed pepper in the oven for 10 minutes, then add the portobello mushroom, asparagus and pecans to the baking tray. Cook for 20 minutes and then remove from oven. Season with salt and pepper, serve with the other half of quinoa salad and pecans crushed and sprinkled on top.

Dinner - Tomato & Basil Soup

- 2 tbsp olive oil
- 1 red onion
- 2 cloves garlic
- 4 large tomatoes
- 1 carrot
- 1 celery stick
- Handful of basil leaves
- Fresh thyme and sage
- ½ pint bouillon
- 2 tbsp tomato puree
- 1 tsp coconut sugar
- Salt & pepper

Chop the vegetables into small pieces. Heat the oil in a pan, add onions and garlic, cook for a few minutes, add carrot and celery. Mix well, then add tomato puree, tomatoes, basil, thyme, sage, salt, pepper, sugar and bouillon. Give it a good stir.

Bring to the boil then reduce to simmer. Cook for 20 minutes. Allow the soup to cool down a little before blitzing it in a blender. Put it back into the pan, re-heat and serve garnished with pepper and some basil leaves.

Evening Sadhana

Savasana – Corpse Pose

Savasana is a wonderful pose to do at the end of a busy day. It is deeply relaxing and restores balance to the body and mind. Corpse pose promotes healing and deep sleep.

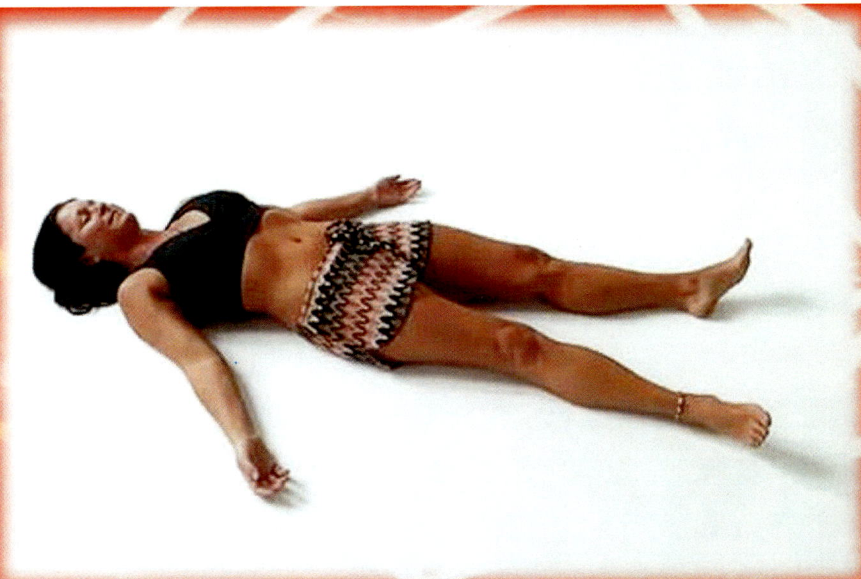

Lie down on your back and let your hips and feet naturally roll out to the sides so your legs are completely relaxed. Place your arms slightly away from the body palms facing upwards to encourage the energy to flow freely around the body. Make sure your shoulders are relaxed and down away from your ears. Scan your body for tension, and if you find any, direct the breath into that area and let it go. Practice deep abdominal breathing and with every exhalation, feel your body completely relax. Feel the heaviness of your body sinking deep into the Earth, relaxing deeper with each breath. Stay in savasana for 5 - 10 minutes and then go straight to bed to reap the benefits of a deep peaceful sleep.

Day 2 – Let Go & Flow...

"I am Creative, and in the Flow"

Pelvic Circles

Pelvic circles are great for freeing up energy within the sacral chakra and awakening the creative life force energy. It gets the energy flowing all the way up the spine to nourish the brain and is good for alleviating stress and tension. It is easy to get lost in this movement, which brings us into the present moment, and the creative flow of life.

Begin in sukhasana, and bring awareness to swadhistana, visualising a bright orange ball of energy swirling around your pelvis. Start to make spirals with your body. Inhale as you spiral forward from the navel point, opening your heart. Exhale as you spiral backward, rolling through one hip and then the other. Continue with the circles and allow your movements to be rhythmic and flowing.

With your eyes closed, turn your gaze upwards towards your third eye. As you circle your body, tune into the energy of swadhistana and the orange glowing energy shining within your pelvic bowl. Practice for 1 minute this way then change direction. Repeat twice on both sides.

Standing Energy Flow

Time to get your groove on! This flow is great for boosting your energy levels and perfect for first thing in the morning to wake up the body and mind. It is a good technique to use when you need to get rid of negative energy or toxic thoughts and feelings.

From mountain pose, shift your weight to your right leg and find your balance, you may hold onto a wall or chair if needed. Rotate your ankle 3 times in each direction. Gently shake your ankle to get the energy moving, then increase the movement by kicking the leg forward away from the body. Imagine you are kicking away the negative energy of anything you want to release from your life. Let go of the old to make room for the new.

Spend 1 minute shaking it out and kicking away, then come back into mountain pose and notice how the right leg feels compared to the left. Repeat on the other side. Now the legs are feeling energised and awake, let's do the same with the upper body.

Start by rotating your right wrist 3 times in each direction. Now shake it out in all directions, feeling it loosening up. Bend your elbow and flick the arm away from the body, visualising you are releasing tension from the mind. Keep shaking and flicking the arm. After a minute stop, and notice how the right arm feels compared with the left. Repeat on other side. To finish the sequence, shake out your whole body as fast as you can for 30 seconds. The energy you feel, the tingling sensations, is your energy body and you can control your energy at will. Whenever you feel tired or low in energy, do this to give yourself a boost.

Swadhistana Cleanse

Carrot & Orange Juice

- 2 large oranges
- 1 carrot, diced
- 1 inch ginger
- ¼ tsp turmeric

Juice the oranges, carrot and ginger, pour into a glass, add turmeric and mix well. Visualise the orange juice awakening your creative energies of swadhistana.

Lunch – Dahl Handi

- 1 cup yellow dahl
- ½ litre bouillon
- 1 tbsp coconut oil
- 1 onion, chopped
- 2 carrots, diced
- 2 cloves garlic, minced
- 2cm fresh ginger, chopped
- ½ tsp turmeric
- ½ tsp garam masala
- 1 tsp curry powder
- ½ tsp cinnamon

Wash and rinse the dahl. Boil the bouillon, add dahl and reduce to simmer for 30 minutes. Heat oil in a separate pan and add onions for 5 minutes, then add garlic, ginger and all the spices mixing well. Stir carrots into the pan, add the dahl and extra water if needed. Simmer for 20 minutes. Serve with basmati rice or chapati, and garnish with coriander.

Dinner - Carrot & Coriander Soup

- 2 carrots, chopped
- ¼ cup orange lentils
- 1 shallot, chopped
- 2 cloves garlic, minced
- 1 inch ginger, chopped
- 1 tbsp coconut oil
- ½ litre bouillon
- 2 handfuls of coriander
- Salt & pepper

Heat the oil in a pan, add onions and cook until soft. Stir in garlic, ginger and carrots and cook for 1 minute. Add the lentils, bouillon, salt and pepper, bring to the boil then reduce the heat. Cook for 45 minutes until the lentils are cooked. Allow it cool down, then add half to the blender along with coriander and blitz until smooth. Add back into the pan and re-heat. Garnish with fresh coriander leaves and enjoy!

Evening Sadhana

Reclining Butterfly Pose

This is a great pose for relaxing the body and mind. It is a gentle hip opener that encourages apana flow to release tension and blockages from the sacral and root chakras. It is a good stretch for the groin, adductors and knees.

From savasana, slowly and mindfully bring your feet together and allow your hips to relax out to the side away from the body. If this is uncomfortable or painful in the hips, place blankets or cushions under the hips and knees for support. Place one hand on your lower abdomen and the other on your chest. Focus on your breathing taking slow deep breaths. Feel your body relaxing, sinking deeper into the pose with each exhalation. Completely relax into the pose and allow gravity to open your hips. To release, bring your hands to knees and gently lift back to centre. Avoid this pose if you have a hip injury.

Day 3 – Step into Your Power

"I am Powerful"

Ardha Matsyendrasana – Half Lord of the Fishes Pose

This pose releases tension from the spine, strenthens the abdominal and oblique muscles and stretches the hips, neck, shoulders and chest. This is a great pose for stimulating manipura and the digestive fire.

Spend a few moments sat in sukhasana and focus on manipura.

Visualise a vibrant yellow ball of energy as bright as the sun emanating from your solar plexus chakra as you connect with your Divine power.

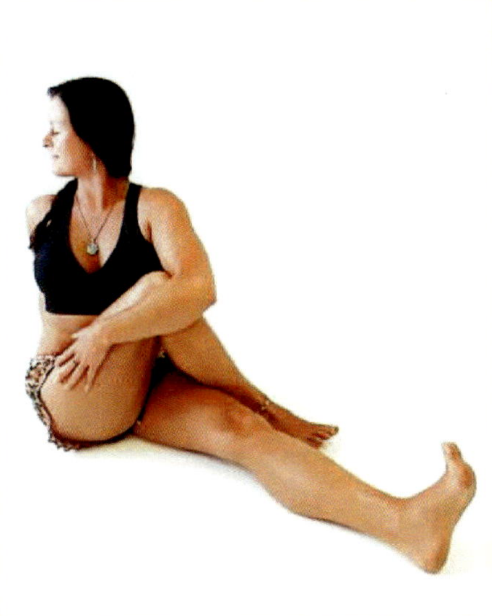

From a seated position, extend your legs out in front of the body. Sit tall and lengthen through the spine. Bend the right leg and place it on the outside of the left leg close to the body. Place your right hand on the floor behind the body and hug the right knee with the left arm. Inhale and lengthen through the spine. As you exhale, twist the body and look over your right shoulder. Hold for 5 breaths and slowly untwist as you exhale. Extend both legs out in front of the body and sit with the spine erect for a few breaths to realign the spine. Repeat on the other side. Avoid this pose if you have had a recent hip or lower back injury.

<u>Top 3 Poses for a Healthy Spine & Digestion</u>

This sequence is fantastic for improving the posture and strengthening the spine and digestive system.

Utthita Tadasana: This variation of mountain pose is a great stretch for the whole body from head to toes. It relieves tension from the back and shoulders and realigns the spine. The gentle stretching of the abdomen improves digestion and tones the abominal muscles and organs.

Begin in mountain pose with your feet hip distance apart. Reach arms overhead and interlace your fingers palms facing upwards, and rest them on your head. Focus your gaze on one fixed point in front of you. As you inhale, reach your arms up to the sky and come up onto your tip toes. Feel your entire body opening up as you stretch as high as you can. Exhale and come back to the starting position with your feet firmly grounded into the Earth. Repeat 6 - 11 times.

Tiryak Tadasana: A great stretch for the whole body, relieving tension from the back, neck, shoulders, pelvis and stomach area. It gently stimualtes manipura and is good for digestion.

Stand tall with your feet slightly wider than hip distance apart. Reach both arms overhead and interlace your fingers palms facing upwards, arms extended towards the sky. Make sure your shoulders are relaxed and down away from the ears. Inhale and lengthen through the spine. As you exhale, bend to the right slightly, keeping your body in a perfectly straight line – do not let your body lean forward or backwards; imagine you are between 2 panes of glass and you can only move in one direction. It doesn't matter how small the movement is, the important thing is to really focus on alignment. This will flush out toxic waste from the intervertebral discs and encourage nutrients and oxygen to enter. Inhale as you come back to centre, lengthening through the spine. Exhale and repeat on the other side. Practice 6 times of each side.

Kati chakrasana: is a strong grounding pose that strengthens the legs and knees, improves flexibility in the spine and releases tension from the spine and back muscles. The twisting action stimulates manipura and improves digestion.

Stand with your feet the width of your yoga mat (roughly 2 hip distances apart) and soften your knees. Extend your arms away from the body parallel to the floor. Inhale and lengthen through the spine, reaching the arms away from each other. Feel the energy surge from your core down your arms and out through the fingertips. As you exhale, twist to the right, bringing your right hand to left side of your lower back palm facing outwards, and left hand on top of right shoulder parallel to the ground, whilst looking over your right shoulder. Inhale as you untwist and come back to centre. Lengthen through the spine and reach your arms away from your body. Exhale and repeat on the other side. Continue for 6 repetitions each side.

Manipura Cleanse

Totally Tropical Smoothie

- ¼ pineapple, diced
- ½ mango, diced
- ¼ inch ginger, grated
- ½ lemon, juiced
- ¼ cup of coconut water

Pop all ingredients in a blender and enjoy your totally tropical smoothie sat outside in the sunshine if possible.

Lunch - Pineapple Kitcheri

- ½ cup yellow lentils
- ½ cup basmati rice
- 1 pineapple
- 1 pint bouillon
- 1 tbsp coconut oil
- ½ tsp cumin seeds
- 1 red onion, chopped
- 2 cloves garlic, minced
- 1 tsp turmeric
- 1 tsp cinnamon
- Salt & pepper
- ½ cup peas
- ½ brocolli, chopped
- Handful cashew nuts
- Handful raisins
- Fresh mint leaves

Cut the pineapple lengthways and slice a grid to scoop out the insides and put to the side for later. Heat the coconut oil in a large pan and add cumin seeds until they pop and sizzle. Add the onion, saute until golden, then add garlic and mix together. Add dahl and bouillon to the pan and cook for 30 minutes. Next, add the rice, peas, brocolli, turmeric, cinnamon, salt, pepper and raisins and stir well. Bring to the boil, reduce to a low heat and cook for 15-20 minutes. Add cashew nuts and pineapple chunks towards the end of cooking and mix in well. Serve inside the pineapple and garnish with fresh mint leaves.

Dinner - Curried Sweetcorn Soup

- 1 cup sweetcorn
- 1 shallot, finely chopped
- 2 cloves garlic, minced
- 1 potato, cut into small cubes
- 1 tbsp coconut oil
- 1 litre bouillon
- 1 tsp curry powder
- Fresh chives, chopped
- Salt & pepper

Heat the oil in a pan and cook the shallot for 5 minutes until softened. Add garlic, potatoes and sweetcorn, stir well and cook for 2 minutes. Then add the bouillon and curry powder, bring to the boil and reduce to a low heat. Simmer for 10 minutes until the potato has cooked. Season with salt and pepper and pour into a blender, blitzing until smooth. Serve garnished with fresh chives.

Evening Sadhana

Reclining Twist

This pose stimulates manipura, balancing the fire within. It realigns and lengthens the spine and sides of the body. It also stimulates and detoxifies the digestive organs, improving digestion.

From reclining butterfly pose, bring your knees and feet together and extend your arms out in a straight line with your palms facing up. Inhale deeply and fully, on the exhalation, slowly lower your knees to the right, turning your head to the left. Feel your body relaxing into the twist with every outbreath. Stay for a minute on this side, then inhale and bring your knees to centre. Repeat on the other side. Once you have done both sides, hug your knees into the chest then rest in savasana.

Day 4 – Air – Restore Balance

"I am Love"

Marjaryasana/Bitilasana - Cat/Cow

This spinal flow increases flexibility of the whole spine, opens all the chakras and is great for rising the energies up from the lower chakras into the heart. It opens the chest and upper back muscles, freeing up tension from around the heart chakra area.

Begin in tabletop with wrists under shoulders and knees under your hips. Firmly press your hands into the ground. Inhale and tilt your pelvis downwards so your stomach is closer to the floor. Open your chest, shoulders and heart centre as you gently take your head back and look up towards your third eye. As you exhale, lower your chin to your chest and curl up through your spine, arching your back into cat pose. Inhale to cow pose, and exhale to cat pose, repeat 6 times. Avoid if you have excessive curvature of lower back. Keep your head in alignment with your torso rather than taking it back if you have a neck injury.

Standing Angel Wings

Angel wings are a wonderful way to open your heart to love and freedom. It gently opens all the chakras allowing the energy to move freely up and down the spine, with a strong emphasis on the heart chakra. This movement will heal your wings and set your soul free.

From mountain pose, bring your hands together into namaste mudra in front of the heart. Inhale and open your big beautiful angel wings. Feel the energy emanating from your heart chakra, radiating down your arms and out of your palms and fingertips. Stay here for a few breaths, or as long as you wish. When you are ready, take a deep breath in and feel the emerald green light flowing into your heart chakra and around your whole body. As you exhale, stretch the arms, palms and fingertips out wide as you scoop your angel wings around your body, enveloping yourself with a warm loving embrace. Inhale to open your angelic wings, and exhale to wrap them around you. Play with your wings and listen to your body and what it is communicating to you as you fly free.

Anahata Cleanse

Avocado Magic Smoothie

- Handful of spinach
- Handful of kale
- ½ avocado
- 2 dates, chopped
- ½ cup almond milk
- Small sprig of mint

Blitz together all the ingredients in a blender and serve garnished with fresh mint.

Lunch - Super Greens Salad

- Handful of spinach & kale
- Handful of rainbow chard
- Hanful of green olives
- 1 green apple, diced
- ¼ small cucumber, sliced
- ½ avocado
- ¼ carrot, grated
- Handful of pine nuts

For the dressing, add ½ tsp balsamic vinegar, 1 tsp hemp oil, ½ tsp mustard and ½ lime to a bowl and mix well. Mix together all ingredients in a large salad bowl. Pour the dressing evenly over the salad and give it another good mix. Serve and enjoy in nature, go on, get outside, you deserve it!

Minty Asparagus, Spinach & Broccoli Soup

- 2 tbsp coconut oil
- 1 onion, finely chopped
- 1 clove of garlic, finely chopped
- 1 inch of ginger, grated
- 200g asparagus, finely chopped
- 1 broccoli head
- Large handful of spinach
- 2 handfuls of fresh mint leaves
- ½ litre bouillon
- Salt & black pepper
- 2 tbsp coconut cream

Heat the oil in a pan over a medium heat. Add the onion and cook for a few minutes until softened. Add the garlic, ginger, broccoli, spinach and asparagus, mix well and cook for another 2 minutes. Add the bouillon and bring to the boil. Season with salt and pepper and then reduce the heat to simmer for 10 minutes until the vegetables are cooked through. Allow to cool, add to the blender along with the coconut cream and mint and blitz until smooth. Put back into the pan and re-heat. Pour into a bowl and using a small spoon, add a little coconut cream to the centre and circle around the bowl to make a fancy pattern. Serve garnished with fresh mint leaves.

Evening Sadhana

Supported Savasana

This variation of savasana is a deeply nourishing heart opener that will enable the energies to flow freely through the heart. It is a great pose for calming the nervous system and restoring balance within. You will need a few blankets or bolsters.

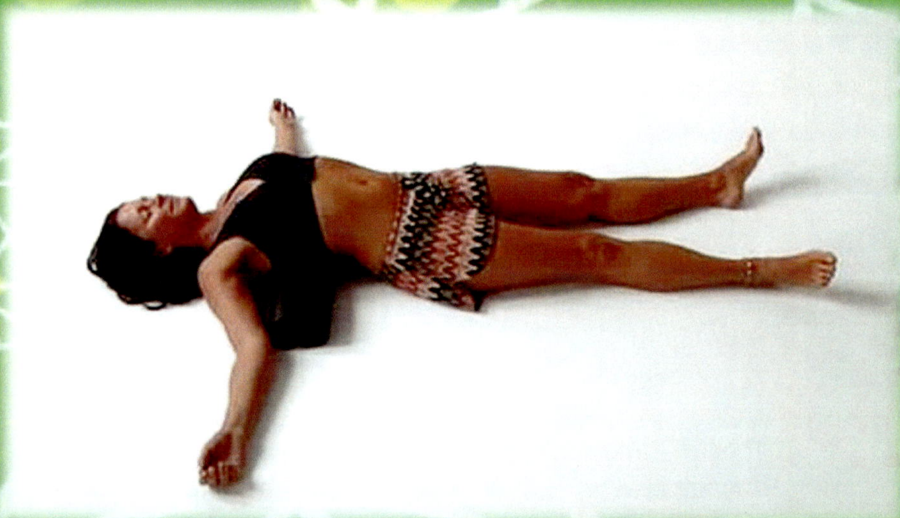

Use a bolster if you have one, or roll up your yoga mat and position it underneath your shoulder blades. Slowly lie back over the rolled up mat and come into savasana with the arms open and relaxed out by the sides of the body. The hips, knees and feet should be open and relaxed. You can also place a rolled up blanket under the knees for extra comfort and support. Breathe deeply into your heart, and feel it expand with love as you visualise an emerald green light shining brightly in the centre of your chest. Exhale, feel yourself let go... Feel the whole body relax and soften. Surrender into the Earth, relaxing deeper and deeper with each breath. Stay here for 5 blissful minutes, savouring each breath.

Day 5 – Space – Express Your Truth

"I am Authentic"

Neck Rotations in Vajrasana (Hero Pose)

Vajrasana is a powerful pose that calms the mind, stretches the legs and feet, and strengthens the digestive system. Neck rotations are good for releasing blockages in the throat chakra and tension from the upper back, neck and shoulders.

From cat/cow, sit back onto your heels and lengthen through the spine. Roll your shoulders back and down, opening through the chest and heart centre. Place your palms facing downwards on your thighs. Inhale deeply, and as you exhale lower your chin to your chest opening through the back of the neck and upper back. Inhale and rotate your head to the right and back. Exhale to complete the second half of the circle as your head comes down towards the chest. Move slowly and mindfully. Repeat 3 times in both directions. Avoid if you have neck injury.

Lion's Breath

This pose is really good for opening up the throat chakra and releasing built up tension and emotions from the system.

Standing in mountain pose, create a strong foundation through your feet. Allow your whole body to relax completely. Inhale, breathe deeply and fully, feel the life force energy opening your body, rising up from the base of spine into your throat. As you exhale, open your mouth and stick out your tongue as far as you can, making an 'ahhhh' sound, take your gaze up towards your third eye. Relax and feel the energy in your face and throat.

To release stress and negativity, think of something you want to release and visualise it in your palms. Make a first and feel the emotion fully as you tense up your whole body. As you exhale, imagine you are throwing the energy out of the body as you flick your hands open and do lions breath at the same time. This is a powerful technique, only practice 3 times.

Vishuddhi Cleanse

Blueberry & Coconut Smoothie

- 2 handfuls of blueberries
- ½ cup coconut milk
- ½ tsp blue spirulina
- Fresh mint leaves

Blitz blueberries, coconut milk and blue spirulina together in a blender. Garnish with fresh mint leaves and a few blueberries on top.

Lunch - Blue Magic Smoothie Bowl

- 2 handfuls of blueberries
- 1 banana, chopped
- 1 handful of spinach
- 1 tsp chia seeds
- 1 tsp blue spirulina powder
- ¼ cup coconut milk
- 2 tbsp oats
- 1 tbsp raisins
- 1 tbsp mixed nuts & seeds
- Handful of fresh fruit

Blend the blueberries, banana, spinach, chia seeds, blue spirulina and coconut milk into a thick smoothie. Mix together the oats, raisins, nuts and seeds. Pour the smoothie into a bowl and top with the homemade muesli mix. Add extra blueberries and other fruits on top. Enjoy with a warm drink.

Dinner - Blue Magic Soup

- 1 leek, diced
- 2 carrots, diced
- 1 celery stick, diced
- 2 handfuls of baby potatoes, quartered
- ½ onion, chopped
- 2 cloves of garlic, minced
- 1 inch of ginger, grated
- 1 tbsp coconut oil
- Fresh herbs: chives, marjoram, thyme, sage and curry leaves
- Dry herbs: oregano, basil and mint
- Salt & pepper
- 1 tbsp blue spirulina

Heat the oil in a pan, add onion, garlic and ginger, cook for 5 minutes. Add the fresh herbs and mix into the pan along with the vegetables. Add the dry herbs and mix together well. Cook for 20 minutes. Add salt and pepper to taste. Remove from the heat and allow to cool. Put half the soup and blue spirulina in a blender to liquidise into a thick consistency. Pour back into the pan and re-heat. Voila! There you have a delicious Blue Magic Soup!

Evening Sadhana

Chanting

Chanting is amazing for opening the throat chakra. It is an empowering practice that immediately lifts your energy and mood, boosting physical, mental and emotional health. It helps to release blockages from the body and mind.

Sit in sukhasana, or any other comfortable seated position. Starting from the base of your spine, chant the biji mantras for the 7 chakras 3 times each.

LAM – VAM – RAM – YAM – HAM – AUM – AUM (silently)

Keep your awareness on the chakra you are chanting, and visualise the corresponding colour, feeling it glowing luminously within your spine. As you move up through the chakras, see the rainbow colours shining from the base of the spine all the way up to the crown of your head. Feel your connection to the whole Universe through your energy body... You are the Rainbow Bridge, manifesting Heaven on Earth.

Day 6 – Light – Inner Peace

"I am Peaceful"

Balasana - Child Pose

Child pose is deeply restorative for the body and mind. It provides a gentle stretch to the spine, and is good for digestion. It soothes the nervous system and stimulates the pineal gland.

From vajrasana, place your hands on the floor and slowly lower your chest to the ground extending your arms forward. Press your palms firmly into the ground and away from the body, encouraging your hips to sit closer to your heels. Place your forehead on the ground, or if you cannot reach, use a block or cushion. Feel the gentle stimulation of the third eye chakra soothe your mind, bringing you into a state of peacefulness and serenity. As you exhale, feel yourself let go, sinking deeper and deeper into tranquility with each breath. Stay in the pose for a few minutes and slowly release.

Vrikshasana: Tree Pose

Vrikshasana is a strong grounding pose that builds strength in the core, legs, knees and ankles. It improves balance and coordination between the brain and body, and also strengthens the immune system. This is a great pose for developing focus, concentration and enhacing spiritual awareness.

Begin in mountain pose, with a strong foundation. Focus your gaze on one fixed point and shift the weight over to your right leg. Open your left hip and turn your knee out to the side, resting your left heel on the inner edge of your right foot with the ball of your foot and toes on the ground. Once you feel stable and grounded, lift your left foot and place it on the inner edge of your calf, lightly on the inner edge of your knee, or if you are more flexible, place the foot firmly on your inner thigh. Bring your hands together in front of your chest. Focus on grounding your standing leg into the Earth, creating stability and strength through your whole body. Activate mulabandha for extra power and to ignite your core strength.

Once you feel strong and grounded in tree pose, you can play around with different arm variations. Use your imagination and think of all the many kinds of trees you can pretend to be. I love playing around with palm tree pose, swaying from side to side, feeling the ocean breeze flowing through my branches and blowing my leaves in the wind.

If your balance needs a bit of work, you can develop strength and stability by pretending that you are a solid oak tree, visualising your roots thick and strong growing deep into the Earth. With each out breath you become more grounded as you strengthen your foundations to your physical body and Mother Earth.

You can hold onto a wall for support and to stabilise yourself while in this asana. Avoid this pose if there is any knee pain.

Ajna Cleanse

As we move into the higher chakras, the vibrations are faster and more subtle, we require less food. Today's cleanse will prepare you for your fast tomorrow. Enjoy a delicious beetroot smoothie for breakfast, and have your lunch a little later today if possible as you will be replacing dinner with golden milk.

Beetroot Smoothie

- 1 beetroot, diced
- 1 celery stick, chopped
- 1 apple, chopped
- ½ cup coconut water
- Handful of mint leaves

Put all ingredients into a blender and mix on high power until everything is smooth. Garnish with mint and enjoy.

Lunch - Roasted Beetroot Soup

- 2 beetroots, diced
- 1 carrot, diced
- 1 leek, chopped
- ½ pint bouillon
- 1 tbsp coconut oil
- 1 red onion, chopped
- 1 clove of garlic, minced
- ½ tsp fresh thyme
- 1 tbsp lemon juice
- Salt & pepper
- 1 tsp pumpkin seeds

Pre-heat the oven to 200C. Put the beetroot and carrots in a baking dish and season with salt and pepper. Roast for one hour and set aside to cool. Heat the oil in a pan, stir in the onion, garlic and leek. Cook for around 5 minutes, then mix in the vegetables, bouillon and thyme. Bring to the boil and then reduce the heat.

Cook for around 15 minutes. Remove from the heat and allow the soup to cool down before blending until smooth. Mix in the lemon juice and re-heat if needed. Garnish with grated carrot and beetroot with mint and pumpkin seeds.

Dinner - Golden Milk

- 1 cup almond milk
- ½ tsp turmeric
- ¼ tsp cinnamon
- Dash of nutmeg
- Dash of cayenne pepper
- Dash of black pepper
- 6 cardamom pods
- 1 cinnamon stick

Bring the almond milk to boil in a saucepan then reduce the heat. Crush the cardamom pods to release the seeds and delicious aroma. Mix the spices into the pan one at a time, stirring in between. Simmer on a low heat for 15 minutes. Strain the milk into your favourite cup to remove the cardamom pods. Pop a cinnamon stick in your cup and enjoy this delicious elixir in a meditative frame of mind to induce a deep restorative sleep. Set your intention to wake up feeling revitalised and full of vitality.

Evening Sadhana

Tratak

Tratak is a practice of dharana that focuses the eyes and the mind on one fixed point, finding stillness in the body and mind. It can be done with a black dot or candle flame. The light of the flame stimulates the development and functioning of the pineal gland and activates the third eye chakra, developing intuition and clairvoyancy.

Prepare the room by making it dark, and place a candle about 25 inches away from your face with the flame at eye level. You can use a yoga block or cushion to sit on. Come into sukhasana or any comfortable seated position, or you can sit on a chair if you prefer. Light your candle and focus on deep abdominal breathing to relax the body and prepare the mind.

Fix your gaze on the candle flame and focus all your attention on the flame. If any thoughts arise, let them go and bring awareness back to the flame. Maintain your gaze as long as you can. If your eyes start to water, close them and visualise the candle in your mind's eye. Feel the peaceful energy of tratak permeate your entire being. Practice for up to 5 minutes. Avoid if you have eye problems or weakness of the eyes.

Day 7 – Sound – Be Still & Listen

"I am Divine"

Adho Mukha Svanasana: Downward Facing Dog Pose

This posture lengthens and stretches the whole back line of the body. It is an energising pose that is great for improving posture and eliminating stiffness, especially in the upper back. This gentle inversion encourages blood to flow to the brain, and energy to flow from the lower to higher chakras.

From tabletop position, place hands a few inches in front of the shoulders and spread your fingers wide with the middle fingers pointing forwards. Press down through all four corners of each palms and the tips of the fingers to create a strong foundation to the Earth.

With your feet hip distance apart, tuck your toes under, and on inhalation, lift your hips up towards the sky. Keep your knees bent at first and extend your hips to the sky. As you exhale, lower your heels towards the ground and straighten your legs if it feels comfortable. Shift the weight into your hips and legs. Your heels should point backwards, if you can see them when you look back try turning them slightly.

Press your hands firmly into the ground and internally rotate your forearms, feeling the energy moving from the Earth up the arms. Externally rotate the upper arms from the shoulder to create space in the upper back and torso. Keep your neck in a neutral position with your ears aligned with your upper arms. Gaze towards your navel. Visualise the energy flowing from the base of the spine, moving through all the chakras and out through the crown of the head.

Avoid this pose if you have any wrist injury or high blood pressure.

Uttanasana: Standing Forward Fold

This is a great pose to calm the mind, relieving stress, anxiety, depression, fatigue, headaches and insomnia. It grounds the body and strengthens the legs. The lower back, hips, hamstrings and calves are stretched and the abdominal organs are stimulated, improving your digestion.

From downward facing dog pose, walk your feet to the top of your mat. Place the feet hip distance apart and soften your knees. Allow your body to naturally fold forward and focus on the lower back opening up. Take hold of the opposite elbow and stay here for a few breaths. Each time you exhale, allow yourself to relax deeper into the pose. Sway from side to side and visualise any tension rolling off the spine, shoulders and neck into the Earth. Stay for several breaths before moving onto the next pose.

If bending forward causes you discomfort, avoid this pose. The deeper you bend your knees in this forward fold, the more the stretch is emphasised in the lower back and sacrum, releasing built up tension.

From uttanasana, keep your knees bent and place your hands on your shins or thighs. Inhale and lengthen through your spine, creating space between the vertebra. As you exhale, slowly press your feet firmly into the ground, keeping your knees bent and start to roll up one vertebra at a time, keeping your chin on your chest until your spine is fully erect. Once standing tall, roll your shoulders back and down, chin parallel to the ground.

Stand strong in mountain pose, and visualise the energy rising up from the Earth, into the soles of your feet, moving all the way up your legs. As the energy moves into your root chakra, breathe deeply into the pelvic floor. Exhale, release the breath, contract mulabandha and draw the navel in towards your spine and up to your heart. Feel the energy move all the way up your spine out through the crown of your head. Feel the liberation current of the kundalini energy opening up sushumna channel and infusing your body with light.

Visualise the light flowing out of the crown chakra and around the body, so that your body is bathed and cocooned in blissful energy.

Sahasrara Cleanse

During your fast today, drink plenty of fluids. If you are doing a mono-fast, I recommend watermelon, apple or pear. If you are breaking your fast at dinner time, have a delicious bowl of detoxifying mung bean soup.

Detoxifying Mung Bean Soup

- ½ cup green mung beans, washed and soaked
- ½ tsp turmeric
- 1 litre of water
- 1 tsp bouillon powder
- 1 tsp coconut oil
- ¼ tsp asafoetida
- 1 tsp cumin seeds
- 1 tsp fennel seeds
- 1 tsp ginger, grated
- ½ tsp garam masala
- Salt & black pepper
- 1 tbsp fresh coriander

Wash the mung beans several times then soak overnight or for at least 4 hours before cooking. Bring the water to the boil and add the bouillon powder. Add mung beans and turmeric, simmer for around 30 minutes. Heat the oil in a separate pan, add the asafoetida and sizzle for 5 seconds. Add the cumin and fennel seeds and cook for 30 seconds until the seeds start to pop. Add the ginger, garam masala and black pepper, let them sizzle for 20 seconds and then add the mung beans to the pan stirring everything well. Simmer for 20 minutes and add salt to taste. Serve with fresh coriander and lemon juice.

Evening Sadhana

Yoga Nidra

Yoga nidra means yogic sleep, it is a deeply restorative practice that will nourish your body, mind and soul. This relaxing form of meditation improves the functioning of the nervous and endocrine systems. You are in a state between being awake and asleep, and the mind is extremely receptive. Yoga nidra helps you to gain power over your mind. Regular practice will help you to change your thought patterns, create new ways of thinking and develop healthy habits.

Yoga nidra is a guided meditation, it isn't possible for you to practice this without a voice recording. Please go to: www.heavenonearth.space/chakra-cleanse and get your free yoga nidra video.

Once you have the link ready, lie on your back in savasana and prepare to enjoy the practice.

Chapter 7: Welcome to the 5th Dimension

What an incredible adventure it is, journeying through the Rainbow Bridge!

I hope you have enjoyed taking this journey with me and that the chakra yoga cleanse has developed more awareness in your life so you can live with more positive energy and less stress.

As I'm sure you've already gathered during your journey through this book, the 5th dimension isn't a place. It is a state of being, a higher level of consciousness. Heaven on Earth is already here in this moment. The 5th dimension is fully active on the planet, with more people attuning to the frequency of higher vibrational energies, choosing in each moment to cultivate Heaven on Earth.

You get to choose what kind of life you want to live and what energy you want to emit.

You are the Creator of your Universe!

You are Magnificent, It Is Your Time to Shine!

Always remember,

You are the Rainbow Bridge between Heaven and Earth

Keep your chakras glowing and magic alive in your heart! Never stop believing in yourself and the dreams that you hold. You are meant to live a spectacular life filled with beauty, romance and love.

Practice self-love daily. Live in your heart centre and be mindful always, it will bring you more joy, peace and happiness. Live your life wholeheartedly and celebrate the majestic being that you are.

Make Health Your Priority

Make health your priority and enjoy Heaven on Earth every single day. Energise your chakras daily with all the techniques you have learned on this cleanse. Play around with recipes and enjoy spending more time in the kitchen. Let this cleanse plan be the foundation for your daily sadhana. Create a routine that you feel excited about so you look forward to your practice every day. I will leave you with this, a beautiful reminder of what to do on a daily basis to raise your vibrations and stay healthy in body, mind, heart and soul. Print a copy of this star and put it in a place where you will see it every day so you can enjoy all the activities that will raise your vibes and keep you in a positive space. Lots of love. Namaste.

^

Sing

Dance

Meditate

Practice yoga

Be more mindful

Eat highly nutritious foods

Be yourself and speak your truth

Drink plenty of water to stay hydrated

< Connect to your Spirit Guides and Angels >

Go for walks outdoors

Spend time in nature

Have a massage

Take time out

Sleep well

Laugh

v

Next Steps on Your Transformational Journey

For more information about the Online Chakra Yoga Cleanse and to receive your *free gifts*, please visit:

https://heavenonearth.space/chakra-cleanse/

All information regarding the bespoke chakra meditation blends can be found on the website using the link above.

To learn more about Sharon's journey and her recovery from a broken back to a life free from pain, check out her previous book; Yoga & Ayurveda: Natural Remedies for Back Pain. You can purchase the book here:

http://ayurvedicyogalifestyle.co.uk/book/

Acknowledgements

I give thanks to the Divine for this wonderful experience called life.

I am eternally grateful for the help I have received in the creation of this book. I would like to thank my family and friends for their support and encouragement, always inspiring me to live my best life. I am thankful to all my students and patients who inspire me every single day, none of this would be possible without you.

My deepest gratitude goes out to all of the teachers at Yoga Vidya Gurukul ashram for their guidance and support on my spiritual journey, their selfless dedication to yoga has been one of the biggest influences in my life. Thank you to Pressiana Vishuddhi for the yantra inspiration whilst taking part in her wonderful chakra studies course during my most recent stay at the ashram, I love the deep meditative state of colouring, it is truly transcendental.

Thank you to Gill Prior for her precise and thought provocative editing, to Holly Candlin for the beautiful yoga photography, Agnes Kocsis (https://www.instagram.com/soulmagicstudio) for her technical and creative talent designing the chakra diagrams, and to Kate Lees and her amazing ability to read my mind and create the most wonderful vibrant images to support my writing. You can find her magical artwork on her Instagram page; https://www.instagram.com/ktdragonflykrafts.

A big shout out to Andrew Crawford and the Write Your Book in 30 days challenge, the daily content and fun filled videos really accelerated the process of bringing this book to life.

A heartfelt thank you to you, the reader. I truly hope this book has inspired you and infused your life with magical energies.

I am deeply grateful for this wonderful life and blessed to share the experience with you all. Thank you for being who you are!

With love, Sharon xxx

Bibliography

Aivanhov, M. Omraam. The Yoga of Nutrition. France: Prosveta S.A., 1990.

Chopra, Deepak. The Complete Book of Ayurvedic Home Remedies London, UK: Piatkus Books, 2006.

Clark, Christopher & Sharma, Hari. Ayurvedic Healing. London, UK: Singing Dragon, 2012.

Collins, Marie. An A-Z Guide to Healing Foods. San Fransisco, CA: Red Wheel/Weiser, 2009.

Frawley, David. Ayurveda and the Mind, The Healing of Consciousness. Twin Lakes, Winconsin: Lotus Press, 1997.

Frawley, David & Lad, Vasant. The Yoga of Herbs.

Hamilton, David. How Your Mind Can Heal Your Body. London, UK: Hay House, 2009.

Holford, Patrick. The Optimum Nutrition Bible. London. UK: Piatkus Books, 2004.

Jelusich, Richard A. Psychology of the Chakras, Eye of the Lotus. Wisconsin, USA: Lotus Press, 2007.

Judith, Anodea. Wheels of Life. Woodbury, MN: Llewellyn Publications, 1999.

Key, Sarah. Back Sufferer's Bible. London, UK: Vermillion, 2000.

Le Blanc, Diane. Welcome to the Fifth Dimension. Berkeley, California: North Atlantic Books, 2010.

Lad, Vasant. Ayurveda, The Science of Self-Healing. Twin Lakes, Winsconsin: Lotus Press, 2009.

McCall, Timothy. Yoga as Medicine. New York: Bantam Dell, 2007.
Pole, Sebastian. A Pukka Life. Bath, UK: Quadrille Publishing Ltd, 2011.

Mother, Sri Aurobindo Ashram, Pondicherry, India: Sri Aurobindo Ashram Publication Department, 2009.

Swami Saraswati, Niramjananananda. Bihar, India: Yoga Publications Trust, 2013.

Swami Saraswati, Satyanananda. Bihar, India: Yoga Publications Trust, 2001.

Dr. Vivekananda, Rishi, Practical Yoga Psychology. Yoga Publications Trust, Ganga Darshan, Munger, Bihar, India, 2005.